30-2641

POVERTY, U. S. A.

THE HISTORICAL RECORD

ADVISORY EDITOR: David J. Rothman

Professor of History, Columbia University

A COMPILATION
OF THE POOR LAWS
OF THE STATE OF PENNSYLVANIA

Pennsylvania, Laws, Statutes, etc.

From the Year 1700 to 1788,

Inclusive

GUARDIANS OF THE POOR

Arno Press & The New York Times
NEW YORK   1971

Reprint Edition 1971 by Arno Press Inc.

LC# 76—137168
ISBN 0—405—03106—8

POVERTY, U.S.A.: THE HISTORICAL RECORD
ISBN for complete set: 0-405-03090-8

Manufactured in the United States of America

A

COMPILATION

OF THE

POOR LAWS

OF THE

S T A T E

O F

PENNSYLVANIA,

From the Year 1700, to 1788, inclusive.

PUBLISHED FOR THE GUARDIANS OF THE POOR.

PHILADELPHIA:
PRINTED BY ZACHARIAH POULSON, JUNIOR, ON THE WEST
SIDE OF FOURTH-STREET, NEAR THE UNIVERSITY.

M DCC LXXXVIII.

A COMPILATION

OF THE

POOR LAWS

OF THE

STATE OF *PENNSYLVANIA.*

An act for the relief of the poor.

[This act was paſſed in the fourth year of Ann, Anno
Domini 1705, and repealed in the eleventh year of
George III, 1771. Province laws, p. 414.]

Overſeers
of the poor
how and
when ap-
pointed.

FOR the better relief of the poor of this
province, *Be it enacted by* JOHN EVANS,
Eſquire, by the queen's royal approbation, lieutenant governor under William Penn,
Eſquire, abſolute proprietary and governor in
chief of the province of Pennſylvania and terri-
tories, by and with the advice and conſent of the
freemen of the ſaid province, in general aſſembly met, and by the authority of the ſame,
That the juſtices of the peace of the reſpective counties of this province, or any three
or more of them, ſhall on the five and twen-
tieth day of March, yearly (unleſs that ſhall
happen on the firſt day of the week) and then
on the day following, meet at ſome convenient
place within their county, and there nominate
and appoint one, two or more (as the caſe
may require) of ſubſtantial inhabitants of the
reſpective townſhips, and where the townſhips
are ſmall and inhabitants few, two or more
(as the juſtices ſhall think fit) may be joined
together within their county, to be overſeers
of the poor of the ſaid townſhips for the year
enſuing.

And

To lay an affeffment, to what a- mount, and how to be employed.

And be it further enaƈted by the authority aforefaid, That it fhall and may be lawful for the overfeer or overfeers of the poor fo no- minated and appointed, to make or lay a rate or affeffment after the rate of one penny per pound, clear value of the real and perfonal eftates of all and every the freeholders and inhabitants within their refpeƈtive townfhips, to be employed for the relief of poor, indi- gent and impotent perfons inhabiting within the faid townfhips, in fuch a manner as by this aƈt is direƈted and appointed; and four fhil- lings per head on all freemen not otherwife rated.

How the overfeers are to pro- ceed in col- lecting the affeffment.

And be it further enaƈted by the authority aforefaid, That the faid overfeers, before they proceed to the colleƈting of the faid rate, fhall procure the fame to be allowed by three or more juftices of the peace of the county wherein the faid tax is made. And if any perfon or perfons fo rated or affeffed, fhall refufe to pay the fum or fums on them charg- ed, that it fhall and may be lawful to and for the faid overfeer or overfeers, having firft ob- tained a warrant under the hands and feals of two juftices of the peace of the county where the faid affeffment is made, who are hereby impowered to grant fuch warrant to levy the fame on the goods and chattels of the perfon or perfons fo refufing; and in cafe fuch perfon fhall not, within three days next after fuch diftrefs made, pay the fum or fums on him af- feffed, together with the charge of fuch di- ftrefs, that the faid overfeer or overfeers may proceed to the fale of the goods diftrained, rendering to the owner the overplus (if any) that fhall remain on fuch fale; reafonable charges firft deduƈted. And in cafe fuch per- fon or perfons have no goods or chattels, whereby

[5]

whereby they may be diftrained, that then it
fhall be lawful for the faid juftices to commit
the offenders to prifon, there to remain without bail or mainprize until they have paid the
fame.

Provided always, That if any perfon or
perfons find themfelves aggrieved with fuch
rate or affeffment, that then it fhall be lawful
for the juftices of the peace, at their next
general quarter feffions, upon petition of
the party, to take fuch order therein as to
them fhall be thought convenient, and the
fame to conclude and bind all parties; and the
overfeer or overfeers fhall forbear fuch diftrefs
till the fame be determined in the quarter
feffions.

*And be it further enacted by the authority
aforefaid,* That the faid overfeers fhall lay the
faid rate according to the beft of their fkill
and judgment, wherein they fhall be guided
by the county affeffment on other occafions,
having due regard to every man's eftate without favor or affection to any.

*And be it further enacted by the authority
aforefaid,* That the father and grand father,
and the mother and grand mother and the
children of every poor, old, blind, lame and
impotent perfon or other poor perfon, not able
to work, being of a fufficient ability, fhall at
their own charges, relieve and maintain every
fuch poor perfon as the juftices of the peace
at their general quarter feffions fhall order and
direct on pain of forfeiting forty fhillings for
every month they fail therein.

*And be it further enacted by the authority
aforefaid,* That it fhall and may be lawful for
the faid overfeers of the poor, by the approbation and confent of two or more juftices of the
peace, to fet on work the children of all fuch

whofe

Appeal to the juftices in feffions, their judgment conclufive.

Overfeers to be guided by the county affeffment.

Fathers & others obliged to maintain poor children, &c.

Overfeers to fet poor children to work and put them out apprentices.

whofe parents fhall not be by the faid juftices thought able to maintain them; and alfo to put fuch children out apprentices for fuch term, as they in their difcretion fhall fee meet.

And be it further enacted by the authority aforefaid, That no perfon or perfons fhall be admitted or entered in the poor's book or receive relief from the overfeers of the poor, before fuch perfon or perfons have procured an order from two juftices of the peace for the fame: And in cafe the faid overfeers fhall enter into their books, or relieve any fuch poor perfon or perfons, without fuch order, they fhall forfeit all fuch money or goods fo paid or diftributed, unlefs the juftices fhall approve and allow them the fame upon making up their accounts.

And be it further enacted by the authority aforefaid, That the juftices of the peace of the faid refpective counties fhall, at leaft ten days before the faid twenty-fifth day of March yearly, iffue out their warrants, directed to the overfeers of the poor of the refpective townfhips within their county, commanding the faid overfeers to appear before them on the faid day and produce their accounts of what money they have received, and difburfed for the ufe of the poor, and alfo to return the names of one or two, or more (as the place may require) of the fufficient inhabitants of the refpective townfhips, to fucceed them in that office for the year enfuing: And in cafe the overfeers fhall neglect to bring in fuch their accounts, as alfo the names of fuch fufficient perfons to fucceed them in that office the year enfuing, fuch perfon or perfons fo neglecting fhall ferve in that office one year longer or otherwife forfeit any fum not exceeding fifty pounds, as the faid juftices fhall think fit

and

Marginal notes:

Overfeers not to grant relief without order under penalty, &c.

Overfeers to fettle their accounts yearly with the juftices and to return the names of one, two or more to fucceed them.

Penalty on neglecting to furnifh their accounts and names of fucceffors.

and direct. And in cafe the perfon or perfons
approved on and appointed by the faid juftices
to be overfeers of the poor of any townfhip
within the refpective counties fhall refufe to
take upon him or them the faid office, and to
do his and their duty therein he or they fhall
forfeit the fum of five pounds each; which Penalty on
faid forfeitures fhall go and be to the ufe of refufing to ferve.
the poor of the town or place where fuch
neglect or refufal fhall be made, and fhall be levied by the conftable, by warrant from any two
juftices of the peace of the faid county, under
their hands and feals, on the goods and chattels of fuch perfon or perfons fo neglecting or
refufing, and by the conftable fold within
three days next after fuch diftrefs made: And
if there happen any overplus upon fale thereof, the fame fhall be paid to the perfon or
perfons to whom the fame fhall belong; reafonable charges firft deduced. And if fuch perfon or perfons, fo neglecting or refufing as
aforefaid, fhall not have goods or chattels,
whereby he or they may be diftrained as aforefaid, that then the faid juftices may commit
the offender or offenders to prifon, there to
remain without bail or mainprize till the faid
forfeitures fhall be by them fully fatisfied and
paid.

*And be it further enacted by the authority
aforefaid,* That the mayor and aldermen of Power of mayor and aldermen.
the city of Philadelphia fhall have the fame
power and authority, by virtue of this act,
within the limits and precincts of their jurifdiction, as well out of feffions, as at their feffions, as is herein limited, prefcribed and appointed to the juftices of the peace of the
county.

An

An act for supplying some defects in the law for the relief of the poor.

[This act was passed in the fourth year of George Ist. Anno Domini 1718, Province laws, p. 96, and repealed the eleventh year of George III. 1771, Province laws, p. 414, but is still in force as to those who obtained settlements under it and have not since acquired new ones.]

WHEREAS by a law of this province, intituled, *An act for the relief of the poor*, it is provided, that the overseers of the poor for the respective townships shall make rates or assessments for the relief of the poor, indigent and impotent persons inhabiting within the said townships, but it is not ascertained what settlements shall render one an inhabitant, relievable by the said act: *Be it therefore enacted by* WILLIAM KEITH, Esquire, by and with the king's royal approbation, deputy-lieutenant and governor under William Penn, Esquire, proprietary and governor in chief of the province of Pennsylvania, &c. by and with the advice and consent of the freemen of the said province, in general assembly met, and by the authority of the same, That where any unmarried person, not having child or children is or shall be lawfully hired as a servant into any city, township or district, in this province and did or shall continue and abide in the same service during the space of one whole year, such service shall be adjudged and deemed a good settlement therein. And if any person shall be bound an apprentice by indenture, and inhabit in any city or township in this province, such binding and inhabiting shall be adjudged a good settlement. And if any person, who hereafter shall come to inhabit in any of the said townships or districts, shall, for himself, and

Settlements of poor persons how obtained.

and on his own account, execute any public annual office or charge in the faid townfhip or diftrict during one whole year, and fhall be charged with and pay his fhare towards the county taxes or levies for the poor of the faid townfhip or diftrict, then he fhall be adjudged and deemed to have a legal fettlement in the fame. And that no other perfon or perfons whatfoever, who fhall come into any county, city, townfhip or diftrict within this province fhall be adjudged to have procured a legal fettlement in fuch county, city, townfhip or diftrict, unlefs he or they fhall really and bona fide take a leafe of a tenement or plantation of the yearly value of five pounds, or unlefs he or they give fufficient fecurity for the difcharge of the faid county, city, townfhip or diftrict, to be allowed by any two juftices of the peace or magiftrates of fuch county or city.

II. *Provided always*, That where any perfon or perfons are come into any county, city, townfhip or diftrict, in this province, out of any other county, city, townfhip or diftrict, or out of any other place or province, and being likely to become chargeable to the place where they are fo come to inhabit, have been or fhall be by required the overfeers of the poor to return from whence they came, or give fecurity for the difcharge of the county, townfhip or place where they are come to inhabit, he, fhe or they refufing and neglecting fo to do, fhall not be deemed to have acquired a legal fettlement by their continuance in the place or places where they are fo come to inhabit, but that upon complaint made by the overfeers of the poor of the proper townfhip or diftrict to any one or more of the juftices of peace or magiftrates of the proper county or city refpectively, where any of the faid perfons (refufing or neglecting to return or give fecurity, or coming to fettle in any tene-

[margin note:] Perfons required to return and not to gain a fettlement by their continuance, but may be removed by warrant unlefs they give fecurity.

B   ment

ment or plantation under the faid yearly value
of five pounds, or not otherwife obtaining a
lawful fettlement, according to the true meaning of this act) fhall refide or be found at the
time of fuch complaint, it fhall and may be
lawful to and for any two juftices of the peace
of the county or city, where any of the faid
perfons who are likely to be chargeable to the
townfhip or place where they refide, or fhall
come to inhabit, by their warrant to remove
and convey fuch perfon or perfons to the county, city, townfhip or place, where he, fhe or
they were laft legally fettled, either as native,
houfeholder, fojourner, apprentice or fervant,
unlefs he or they give fufficient fecurity for the
difcharge of the faid county, city or townfhip;
to be allowed by the faid juftices.

Appeal to the feffions which fhall be conclu- five.   III. *Provided always*, That if any perfon or
perfons fhall find him, her or themfelves aggriev-
ed by any order or determination, which any
of the faid juftices of the peace or magiftrates
fhall make in any of the cafes abovefaid, fuch
perfon or perfons fhall have liberty to appeal
to the next general quarter feffions of the
peace of the county or city, where fuch determination fhall be made, who, upon hearing
of fuch appeal, fhall have full power finally to
determine the fame, and to award cofts, as the
juftices of the peace at their quarter feffions in
Great Britain, by a ftatute made in the eighth
and ninth years of king William the third, are
impowered and required to do in fuch cafes.

IV. And if any perfon be removed by virtue of this act, from one county, city, townfhip or place to another, by warrant, under
the hands and feals of two juftices of the
peace or magiftrates as aforefaid, that the overfeers of the poor of the townfhip or diftrict to
which the faid perfons fhall be fo removed, are
hereby

hereby required to receive the faid perfons: _{Overfeers} And if any of the faid overfeers fhall refufe ^{to receive} or negle& fo to do, he or they fo offending, _{moved into} upon proof thereof by one or more credible _{their coun-} witneffes, upon oath or affirmation, before any _{der penal-} one of the juftices of the fupreme court of ^{ty, &c.} this province, fhall forfeit for each offence the fum of five pounds, to the ufe of the poor of the townfhip or diftri& from which fuch per- fon was removed; to be levied by diftrefs and _{How pe-} fale of the offender's goods, by warrant, under _{be recover-} the hand and feal of the juftices of the faid _{ed and to} fupreme court, which they are hereby impow- ^{whofe ufe.} ered and required to make, dire&ed to the con- ftable of the townfhip where fuch-offender or offenders dwell, returning the overplus, if any be, to the owner or owners: And for want of fufficient diftrefs, then the offender to be committed to the gaol of the county where he dwells, there to remain without bail or mainprize for the fpace of forty days.

V. *Provided always*, That all fuch perfons, _{Appeal to} who think themfelves aggrieved with any fuch _{the quarter} judgment of the faid two juftices, may appeal _{the county} to the next general quarter feffions of the _{from which} peace, to be held for the county or city from _{the pauper} which the faid perfon was fo removed: And _{was remov-} that the appeal againft any order for the re- moval of any poor perfon out of any townfhip or place fhall be had, profecuted and determin- ed at the general quarter feffions of the peace, for the county, city or place from whence fuch poor perfons fhall be removed, doth lie, and not elfewhere.

VI. And to the end, that the monies raifed only for the relief of fuch as are impotent and poor may not be mifapplied and confumed by the idle, fturdy and diforderly beggars, *Be it further enacted by the authority aforefaid*, That
every

every fuch perfon, as from the twenty-fourth
day of June, in this prefent year, one thoufand feven hundred and eighteen, fhall be upon the collection, and receive relief of any
county, city or place and the wife and children of any fuch perfon cohabiting in the fame
houfe (fuch child only excepted as fhall be by
the overfeers of the poor permitted to live at
home, in order to have the care of, and attend

Poor per-
fons reliev-
ed to wear
a badge,
&c.
any impotent and helplefs parent) fhall, upon
the fhoulder of the right fleeve of the upper
garment of every fuch perfon, in an open and
vifible manner, wear fuch badge or mark, as
is herein after mentioned and expreffed; that
is to fay, a large Roman (P.) together with
the firft letter of the name of the county, city
or place, whereof fuch poor perfon is an inhabitant, cut either in red or blue cloth, as by
the overfeers of the poor it fhall be directed
and appointed.

Punifh-
ment for
not wear-
ing a badge
VII. And if any fuch poor perfon fhall at
any time neglect or refufe to wear fuch badge
or mark as aforefaid, and in manner aforefaid,
it fhall and may be lawful for any juftice of the
peace of the county, city or place where any
fuch offence fhall be committed, upon complaint to him for that purpofe made, to punifh
every fuch offender for every fuch offence,
either by ordering of his or her relief, or ufual allowance on the collection to be abridged,
fufpended or withdrawn; or otherwife, by
committing fuch offender to the houfe of correction, there to be whipped, and kept at hard
labor for any number of days, not exceeding
twenty-one, as to the faid juftice fhould feem
meet.

Penalty on
overfeers
relieving
thofe who
do not wear
badges, &c.
VIII. And if any fuch overfeer of the poor
fhall relieve any fuch poor perfon, not having
or wearing fuch badge or mark as aforefaid,
being

being thereof convicted, upon the oath or affirmation of one or more credible witnesses, before any justice of the peace of the county or city where such offence shall be committed, shall forfeit for every such offence the sum of twenty shillings, to be levied by distress and sale of the goods of every such offender, by warrant, under the hand and seal of any such justice; one moiety thereof to the informer, and the other to the poor of the township or place where the offence shall be committed.

A supplement to the several acts of assembly of this province for the relief of the poor.

[This act was passed in the eighth year of George II. Anno Domini 1734, Province laws, p. 181, and repealed in the eleventh year of George III. 1771, Province laws, p. 414.]

WHEREAS it is found by experience, that the laws of this province made for the relief of the poor, and for removing and punishing rogues, vagrants, and other idle and disorderly persons, wandering about the country, have not proved effectual for the good purposes for which they were intended, and for securing the inhabitants of this province from being oppressed with great charges, arising by such idle and disorderly persons, coming from the neighbouring colonies into, and concealing themselves in, the city of Philadelphia, and the respective townships of this province, until they have either gained a settlement, or become so sick and infirm, that they cannot be removed: For remedying which inconveniences, *Be it enacted by* PATRICK GORDON, Esquire, with the king's royal approbation, lieutenant governor under the honorable John Penn, Thomas Penn and Richard Penn, Esquires,

quires, true and abfolute proprietaries of the
province of Pennfylvania, and of the counties
of New Caftle, Kent and Suffex, on Delaware,.
by and with the advice and confent of the reprefentatives of the freemen of the faid province, in general affembly met, and by the au-

No perfon coming into the city, townfhip, &c. to gain a fettlement therein without notice, mariners and other healthy perfons directly from Europe, only excepted. thority of the fame, That no perfon or perfons
whatfoever, coming into the city of Philadelphia,
or into any townfhip or county within this province, mariners and other healthy perfons
coming directly from Europe, only excepted,
although fuch perfon be an hired fervant, and
fhall abide in fuch fervice for the fpace of one
whole year, and although any perfon being
an indented fervant, or be bound apprentice by
indenture in the faid city or in any townfhip
within this province, and fhall continue in fuch
apprenticefhip or fervitude for the fpace of one
year (which is hereby declared fufficient to
gain fuch apprentice and indented fervant a
fettlement, upon notice given as is hereafter
directed in this act, and not otherwife) or although any perfon or perfons fhall, on his own
account, execute any public annual office or
charge in the faid city, or any townfhip within this province, during one whole year, or be
charged and pay his fhare towards the county
taxes or levies for the poor of the faid city or
townfhip, or fhall have bona fide taken a leafe
of a tenement or plantation, of the yearly
value of five pounds or upwards, within the
city of Philadelphia, or any townfhip of this
province, fhall be deemed to have gained a legal
fettlement in the faid city, or in any fuch townfhip, unlefs fuch perfon or perfons fhall, within
five days next after his or her coming into the
city of Philadelphia, or into any townfhip within this province, give notice in writing, which
they are hereby required to do, of the houfe
of

of his or her abode, and the number of his or
her family, if any he or she have, to the respective overseers of the poor, for the time
being, of the said city or township, into which
he or she shall come, nor shall any hired or indented servant or apprentice, by virtue of his
or her being hired, bound or assigned over unto
any person inhabiting the said city, townships or
counties as aforesaid, gain a settlement within
the same, unless notice be given in writing
within ten days after such hiring or binding as
aforesaid, to the overseers of the poor of the
city or township, where such person shall come
to reside, by the person who shall take such apprentice, hire a servant, or purchase an indented servant, or by the person or persons so hired themselves within ten days next after such
hiring; any law, custom or usage, of this province to the contrary in any wise notwithstanding.

II. *Provided always*, That if, upon complaint made by the overseers of the poor of
the city of Philadelphia, or of any township
within this province, to such magistrates as
have a right to hear the same, it shall be adjudged within the space of twelve months next
after such notice, that any person or persons is
or are likely to become chargeable to the city
or township where he or she is come to reside,
and shall upon his or her being required, neglect or refuse to give security, that he or she
shall not become chargeable to the inhabitants
of the said city or township, into which he or
she is come, that then such person or persons
shall be liable to be removed to the last place
of his or her legal settlement, the giving of
notice as aforesaid, or any other thing in this
or any other act of assembly of this province,
to the contrary in any wise notwithstanding.

III. And

Persons likely to become chargeable refusing to give security may be removed, &c.

III. And for the more effectual preventing
rogues, vagabonds, and other idle and diforderly perfons, concealing themfelves within
the faid city of Philadelphia, or in any townfhip or county within this province, *Be it further enacted by the authority aforefaid,* That if
No houfe-
keeper to
entertain
perfons un-
fettled,
without
notice to
the over-
feers. any houfe-keeper or inhabitant of this province
fhall, after the publication of this act, take into,
receive or entertain, in his or her houfe or
houfes, any perfon or perfons whatfoever, healthy mariners and other perfons coming immediately from Europe into the faid province,
only excepted, not being perfons who have
gained a legal fettlement in fome city or townfhip within this province, and fhall not give
notice in writing, which they are hereby required to do, within three days next after the
taking into or entertaining any perfon or perfons in his or her houfe within the city of Philadelphia, to the overfeers of the poor of the
faid city, and within the fpace of ten days next
after his or her taking into or entertaining
any perfon or perfons in his or her houfe, in
any townfhip within this province, to the overfeers of the poor of the townfhip where fuch
perfon dwells, fuch inhabitant or houfekeeper,
being thereof legally convict, by the teftimony
of one credible witnefs, on oath or affirmation, before any two magiftrates of the faid city
of Philadelphia, whereof the mayor or recorder to be one, or before any two magiftrates
of the county where each perfon dwells, fhall
forfeit and pay the fum of twenty fhillings for
every offence, the one moiety to the ufe of the
poor of the faid city or townfhip refpectively,
and the other moiety to the informer, to be
levied on the goods and chattels of the delinquents, in the manner herein after directed;
and for want of fufficient diftrefs, the offender
to

to be committed to the work-houfe of the faid
city or county, there to remain without bail or
mainprize for the fpace of ten days; and moreover, in cafe the perfon or perfons fo entertained or concealed fhall become poor and unable
to maintain him or herfelf, and cannot be removed to the place of his or her laft legal fettlement, or fhall happen to die, and not have
wherewithal to defray the charge of his or
her funeral, then in fuch cafe the houfe-keeper
or perfon, convicted of entertaining or concealing fuch poor perfon againft the tenor of this
act, fhall be obliged to provide for and maintain
fuch poor and indigent perfon or perfons, and
in cafe of fuch poor perfon's death, fhall pay
the overfeers of the poor fo much money as
fhall be expended on the burying of fuch poor
and indigent perfon or perfons; and upon refufal
fo to do, it fhall be lawful for the overfeers
of the poor of the faid city or townfhip refpectively, and they are hereby required to affefs a fum of money on the perfon or perfons
fo convict, from time to time, by a weakly affeffment, for maintaining fuch poor and indigent perfon or perfons, or affefs a fum for defraying the charges of fuch poor perfon's funeral, as the cafe may be; and in cafe the party
convict fhall refufe to pay the fum of money
fo affeffed or charged to the overfeers of the
poor, for the ufes aforefaid, the fame fhall be
levied of the goods and chattels of the offender in the manner herein after directed: But if
fuch perfon fo convicted have no goods or
chattels to fatisfy the money fo affeffed for him
or her to pay, that then it fhall and may be
lawful for the faid juftices to commit the offender to prifon, there to remain without bail or
mainprize, until he or fhe have paid the fame,
or until he or fhe fhall be difcharged by due
order of law.

Under the pain of maintaining them if fick, and burying them if they die.

C   IV. *And*

IV. *And whereas* it is found by experience,
that many poor perfons within this province
cannot find employment in the city or townfhip where they are legally fettled, yet might
find work for themfelves and families in other
places within the province, but not being able
to give fecurity, if required, upon their coming to fettle in any other place, that they and
their families fhall not become chargeable or
burthenfome to any city or townfhip where
they come to dwell, and by that means are
confined to their own city or townfhip, though
their labour may be wanted elfewhere: *Be it
therefore enacted by the authority aforefaid,*
That if any perfon or perfons whatfoever, from
and after the firft day of May, which will be in
the year of our Lord one thoufand feven hundred and thirty-five, fhall come out of the city of Philadelphia, or any townfhip into another townfhip within this province, or fhall
come out of any townfhip in this province into
the city of Philadelphia, there to inhabit and
refide fhall at the fame time procure, bring and
deliver, unto the overfeers of the poor of the
city or townfhip where he or fhe fhall come to
inhabit, a certificate under the hands and feals
of the overfeers of the poor of the city or
townfhip from whence he, fhe or they removed, to be attefted by two or more credible witneffes, thereby acknowledging the perfon or
perfons, mentioned in the faid certificate to
be an inhabitant or inhabitants legally fettled
in that city or townfhip; every fuch certificate,
having been allowed of and fubfcribed by two
or more juftices of the peace of the city or
county where fuch townfhip doth lie, fhall
oblige the faid city or townfhip to receive and
provide for the perfon mentioned in the faid
certificate, together with his or her family, as
inhabitants of that place, whenever he, fhe

*Poor per-
fons remo-
ved into
another
townfhip,
to take a
certificate.*

or

or they fhall happen to become chargeable to,
or be forced to afk relief of, the city or townfhip to which fuch certificate was given, or into which he, fhe or they were received, by virtue of the faid certificate, and then and not
before, it fhall and may be lawful for any fuch
perfon, and his or her children, though born
in the city or townfhip, and his or her
fervants and apprentices, not having otherwife acquired a legal fettlement there, to be
removed, conveyed and fettled, in the city or
townfhip from whence fuch certificate was
brought.

V. *And whereas* it oftentimes happens,
that poor perfons come from the city of Philadelphia into fome townfhip or place within
this province and from fome place or townfhip
of this province into the faid city of Philadelphia, or into fome other townfhip of this province, and conceal themfelves until they become fick or lame, and cannot be removed,
and oftentimes die before they can be removed, by reafon whereof the inhabitants of the
city or townfhip where fuch poor perfon or
perfons fell fick or died are put to charges,
without any means to relieve themfelves from
the payment of the monies, expended upon
the maintenance or burying fuch poor perfon
or perfons, *Be it therefore further enacted by
the authority aforefaid,* That if any poor perfon or perfons fhall come out of the city of
Philadelphia into any townfhip within this province, or fhall come out of any townfhip or
place within this province into the city of Philadelphia, or any other townfhip within this
province, and fhall happen to fall fick or die,
before he or fhe have gained a legal fettlement,
in the city or townfhip to which he or fhe fhall
come, fo that fuch perfon or perfons cannot
be

Overfeers
of the place
of a poor
perfon's
laft fettle-
ment fhall
take care
of him,
when he is
chargeable
to another
townfhip,
place, &c.

be removed, and if, upon notice given by the
overfeers of the poor of the place unto which
fuch poor perfon is come, or by one of them,
to the overfeers of the poor of the city, townfhip or place, where fuch poor perfon or perfons had laft gained a legal fettlement, or to
one of them, of the name, circumftances and
condition, of fuch poor perfon or perfons,
with requeft that they or one of them may
take order for the relief and maintenance of
fuch fick or lame perfon during his or her ficknefs, and for his or her being buried, in cafe
he or fhe fhould die, and if fuch overfeer or
overfeers fhall negleft or refufe fo to do, that
then and in fuch cafe it fhall be lawful for any
two juftices of the peace of the city or county where fuch poor perfon had laft gained a
legal fettlement, and they are hereby authoriz-
ed and required, upon complaint made to them,
to caufe all fuch fum and fums of money, as
fhall be neceffarily expended on the maintenance of fuch poor perfon in his or her ficknefs,
or on his or her burial, by warrant, under
their hands and feals, to be directed to fome
conftable of their county, to be levied by diftrefs and fale of the goods and chattels of the
faid overfeer or overfeers of the poor, fo neglecting or refufing to take care and provide
for any fuch poor perfon as aforefaid, after
fuch notice given to them, or to one of them,
as aforefaid, and to be paid to the overfeer
or overfeers of the city or townfhip where
fuch poor perfon happened to be fick or die as
aforefaid, and the overplus of the monies arifing by fale of fuch goods remaining in the
conftable's hands, after the fum of money ordered to be paid, together with the cofts of
diftrefs, &c. are fatisfied, fhall be reftored to
the owner or owners of the faid goods.

VI. *And*

VI. *And whereas*, by an act of assembly of
this province, intituled, *An act for the relief
of the poor*, it is provided, that it shall and
may be lawful to and for the overseer or overseers of the poor to make and lay a rate of
one penny per pound, clear value of the real
and personal estates of all and every the freeholders and inhabitants within their respective
townships, to be employed for the relief of
the poor, &c. and four shillings per head on
all freemen, not otherwise rated, but it being
found upon experience that the number of the
poor within this province are very much en-
creased, and the overseers of the poor of the
city of Philadelphia, and the respective townships within this province, have been obliged
to lay several rates of one penny per pound in
one year, for maintenance of the poor within
the city of Philadelphia, and the respective
townships within this province, which has
proved very troublesome, as well to the persons on whom the said monies are raised, as to
the persons who are obliged to collect the same:
For the remedying of which inconveniency
for the future, *Be it enacted by the authority
aforesaid*, That it shall and may be lawful to
and for the overseers of the poor of the city
of Philadelphia, for the said city, having first
obtained the approbation of the mayor or recorder, with any two of the aldermen of the
said city, and for the overseers of the poor of
the several townships within this province, having first obtained the approbation of any two
magistrates living next to the township where
any poors tax shall be raised, to make or lay
any rate, not exceeding three-pence in the
pound at one time, upon all the estates liable
to be rated, and in the manner directed to be
raised and levied by the aforesaid act of assembly

Overseers
empower-
ed to in-
crease the
amount of
the rate,
&c.

bly for the relief of the poor, and not exceeding nine shillings per head on all freemen,
not otherwife rated, any thing in the aforefaid
act of affembly, or any other law, cuftom or
ufage, of this province to the contrary in any
wife notwithftanding.

VII. And for the more eafy difcovery,
certain knowledge, and well management of
the affairs of the poor within this province,
and of what monies are raifed for the ufe of
the poor, and to what ufes applied, *Be it fur-*
ther enacted by the authority aforefaid, That
all and every overfeer and overfeers of the
poor of any city or townfhip within this province, fhall, at their laying any rate for the
relief of the poor of their refpective cities or
townfhips, and they are hereby obliged to deliver to one of the juftices of the peace who
allows fuch rate a fair duplicate of the fame,
figned by fuch overfeer, or overfeers, and fhall
likewife deliver to the refpective overfeer or
overfeers, who fhall fucceed them, fair and true
lifts of the poor of their refpective city or
townfhips, with fuch certificates and notices
as fhall be delivered or given to them, upon
the coming of any perfon from the city of
Philadelphia, into any townfhip of this province, or of the coming of any perfon from
any fuch townfhip into the city of Philadelphia, or into any other townfhip within this
province as by this act is provided and directed; for which trouble the juftices are hereby
required to make fuch allowance to the refpective overfeer or overfeers of the poor, within
this province, at their going out of their office,
as to them fhall feem reafonable, for their making fuch duplicates of the rates by them laid,
and for the charge and trouble they may be at
in making fair lifts of their poor, and of the
notices

marginal note: Overfeers to deliver to a juftice a duplicate of the rates laid, and a lift of the poor to their fuc-ceffors, &c.

notices and certificates herein directed to be
delivered to their fucceffors, of which faid
notices and certificates a regifter or entry fhall
be made, by the refpective overfeers of the
poor to whofe hands the fame fhall come, in
a book for that purpofe to be by them provided and kept; which book fhall likewife be delivered by the overfeers aforefaid to the refpective fucceffors in the faid office.

VIII. *And whereas* complaints have been
made againft overfeers of the poor, who have
fupplied the poor with neceffaries out of their
own ftores and fhops at exorbitant prices, and
alfo againft overfeers, who have paid unrea-
fonable accounts to their friends or dependants,
for fervices done to the poor: *And whereas*
the twenty-fifth day of March, appointed by
the aforefaid act for the relief of the poor, is
found by experience not to be a fufficient time
for examining and fettling the accounts of the
feveral overfeers, and for regulating and re-
dreffing the abufes that may be complained
of: *Be it therefore enacted by the authority*
aforefaid, That the magiftrates of the refpective counties, or any three of them, within
this province, for the faid counties, fhall and
may, on the twenty-fifth day of March, and
within three days next after the faid day, and
the mayor or recorder, with any two aldermen
of the city of Philadelphia, for the faid city,
fhall and may, on the faid twenty-fifth day of
March, and at any time within one month after the faid day, annually, examine and fettle
the faid overfeers accounts; and fhall have
full power to allow fuch accounts and fums only, as to them fhall feem juft and reafonable.

IX. *And whereas* the alms-houfe built for
the city of Philadelphia may, if well regulat-
ed, be of fervice, and help to eafe the inhabitants

Overfeers accounts to be examin-ed and al-lowed by the magi-ftrates.

bitants of the taxes yearly affeffed on them for
the maintenance of the poor: *Be it enacted by
the authority aforefaid*, That the mayor and
recorder, with any two or more aldermen of
the faid city of Philadelphia, fhall from time
to time have power and authority to choofe
and appoint a fober and difcreet perfon to refide in the faid alms-houfe, for taking care of
the poor therein, and, where it may be need-
ful, to direct the receiving into the faid alms-
houfe fuch poor, and to employ fuch perfons
in the fervice of the faid houfe, and care of
the poor, and generally to give fuch orders
and inftructions for the well-ordering of the
faid houfe, and the poor of the faid city, as
to the faid mayor and recorder, with any two
or more aldermen of the faid city, fhall feem
juft and reafonable, and to enjoin obedience to
the fame.

Alms-houfe of Philadel-phia, who are to have the govern-ment of it.

X. *And whereas* the overfeers of the poor
of the city of Philadelphia, and the refpective townfhips within this province, at going
out of their office, not only frequently neglect or refufe to deliver to the juftices, a fair
and true account of the monies by them received for the ufe of the poor, but likewife leave
confiderable fums of money, by them affeffed
for the maintenance of the poor, uncollected,
by which means it comes to pafs that the monies remaining uncollected are loft, and the
burthen of maintaining the poor falls heavy
on fuch as have paid their money: For remedying of which inconveniency for the future,
Be it enacted by the authority aforefaid, That
all and every the overfeer and overfeers of the
poor of the city of Philadelphia, and the refpective townfhips within this province fhall, at
their going out of their office, render a fair
and true account to the magiftrates of the city
of

Overfeers to render a fair ac-count at their going out of office to the ma-giftrates, under pe-nalty, &c.

of Philadelphia, for the faid city, and to the juftices of the refpective counties in which they live, of all the monies affeffed by them, or that hath otherwife come to their hands, and how the fame hath be been difpofed of, and alfo what part fhall be remaining in their hands, and to pay the fame to the fucceeding overfeer or overfeers: And if any overfeer or overfeers of any poor within this province fhall refufe or neglect to render fuch account to the juftices as aforefaid, and to pay what fhall be remaining in their hands, according to the direction of the refpective magiftrates, who fhall have the right of examining their accounts, it fhall and may be lawful to and for the faid juftices, or any three of them, to commit fuch overfeer or overfeers to the county goal, without bail or mainprize, until fuch overfeer or overfeers fhall render a true and fair account, and pay fuch monies as fhall appear to be remaining in his or their hands, to the fucceeding overfeer or overfeers of the poor of the faid city or townfhip, to which they refpectively belong.

XI. And if any overfeer or overfeers of the poor of the city of Philadelphia, or of any townfhip within this province, hath or have neglected or refufed, or fhall neglect or refufe, to collect and pay to the fucceeding overfeers, all fuch fums of money as are or fhall be remaining in their hands, or uncollected at their going out of his or their office, which they are hereby enabled to collect, by warrant under the hands and feals of any two magiftrates within the faid city or counties, within the fpace of thirty days after notice, and requeft made to them fo to do, by any juftice of the peace, and being duly convicted thereof before any three juftices of the city or county to

Penalty on overfeers neglecting to collect and pay what is affeffed.

D   which

which they belong, it ſhall and may be lawful
to and for the mayor or recorder, and any two
of the aldermen of the ſaid city, and for any
three juſtices of the peace of the county, in
which ſuch delinquent overſeer or overſeers
dwell, by warrant under their hands and ſeals,
to commit ſuch delinquent overſeer or overſeers to the goal of the county to which they
belong, there to remain, without bail or mainprize, until the ſame ſhall be paid.

XII. And to the end, that the poor may not
ſuffer for want of proper perſons to take due
care of them in their ſicknefs, or neceſſities:
Overſeers *Be it enaſted by the authority aforeſaid*, That
how to be in caſe of the death or want of any overſeer
appointed
in caſe of of the poor of the city of Philadelphia or of
death. any townſhip within this province, it ſhall and
may be lawful to and for the mayor, recorder,
and any two aldermen, or the mayor or recorder with any two aldermen of the city of Philadelphia, for the city of Philadelphia, and any
two juſtices of the peace of the county in which
ſuch townſhip lies, to appoint one or more
overſeers of the poor of the ſaid city or townſhip, as the caſe may require, at any time
when there ſhall be occaſion, which overſeer
or overſeers, when ſo appointed, ſhall be ſub-
jeſt to the ſame rules, and penalties, and obliged to the performance of the ſame duties and
ſervices, as if he or they had been appointed
at the time in the firſt recited aſt of aſſembly
mentioned, any thing in the aforeſaid aſt, or
any law of this province to the contrary in
any wiſe notwithſtanding.

XIII. *And be it further enaſted by the autho-*
Fines and *rity aforeſaid*, That the ſeveral fines, forfeitures
forfeitures and penalties, ſum and ſums of money, impoſ-
how to be
recovered. ed or direſted to be paid by this aſt, and not
herein otherwiſe direſted to be recovered, the
ſame

fame and every of them fhall be levied and recovered by diftrefs and fale of the goods and
chattels of the delinquent or offender, by
warrant under the hands and feals of the
mayor and recorder, or of the mayor or recorder, and one or more aldermen of the city
of Philadelphia, for the faid city, and under
the hands and feals of any two or more juftices
of the peace of the county, where the delinquent or offender dwells, or is to be found;
and after payment or fatisfaction made of the
refpective forfeitures, fines, penalties and fums
of money, directed to be levied by fuch warrant as aforefaid, together with fuch legal
charges as fhall become due in the recovery
thereof, the overplus, if any, to be returned
to the owner or owners of fuch goods or chattels, his or her executors or adminiftrators.

XIV. *Provided always,* That if any perfon
or perfons fhall find him or themfelves aggrieved with any judgment of the juftices, given
out of their feffions, in purfuance of this act,
fuch perfon or perfons may appeal to the next
general quarter feffions of the peace for the
county or city, where fuch judgment or fentence was given, whofe decifion, in all fuch
cafes, fhall be conclufive.

An act for amending the laws relating to the poor.

[Paffed in the twenty-third year of George II. Anno
Domini 1749, Province laws, p. 219. Repealed in
the eleventh year of George III. 1771, Province
laws, p. 414.]

WHEREAS divers perfons within this
province, by their laft wills, or otherwife, may hereafter devife, bequeath, or give
lands, tenements, or fums of money to the ufe
of the poor, and queftions may arife, whether
the

(margin note: Appeal from juftices out of feffions to general quarter feffions.)

the overſeers of the poor can take ſuch gifts, deviſes, or bequeſts, or maintain actions for the ſame:

Lands, &c. given by deed or will to the poor, &c. ſhall paſs to the overſeers; for the uſe of the poor

Be it therefore enacted by the honorable JAMES HAMILTON, Eſquire, lieutenant governor, under the honorable Thomas Penn and Richard Penn, Eſquires, true and abſolute proprietaries of the province of Pennſylvania, and counties of New-caſtle, Kent and Suſſex upon Delaware, by and with the advice and conſent of the repreſentatives of the freemen of the ſaid province, in general aſſembly met, and by the authority of the ſame, That all gifts, grants, deviſes and bequeſts hereafter to be made, of any houſes, lands, tenements, rents, goods, chattels, ſum or ſums of money, not exceeding the yearly value of five hundred pounds, to the poor of any city, borough or townſhip, within this province, or to any other perſon or perſons for their uſe, by deed or by the laſt will and teſtament, of any perſon or perſons, or otherwiſe, howſoever, ſhall be good and available in law, and ſhall paſs ſuch houſes, lands, tenements, rents, goods and chattels to the overſeers of the poor of ſuch city, borough and townſhip, for the uſe of their poor reſpectively.

Overſeers of the poor incorporated

And be it further enacted by the authority aforeſaid, That the ſaid overſeers of the poor for the ſeveral townſhips, city and boroughs aforeſaid, for the time being reſpectively ſhall forever hereafter in name and in fact be, and they are hereby declared to be bodies politic and corporate in law, to all intents and purpoſes, and ſhall have perpetual ſucceſſion, and by the name of overſeers of the poor of the ſaid reſpective townſhips, city or boroughs, may ſue and be ſued, and plead or be impleaded, in all courts of judicature within this province,

vince, and by that name fhall and may purchafe, take or receive any lands, tenements or
hereditaments, not exceeding the yearly value
of five hundred pounds, and alfo any goods
or chattels whatfoever to and for the ufe and
benefit of the poor of each of the faid townfhips, city or boroughs, refpectively, of the
gift, alienation or devife of any perfon or perfons whomfoever, To hold to them the faid
overfeers and their fucceffors in the faid truft,
for the ufe of the faid poor refpectively for
ever.

*And be it further enacted by the authority
aforefaid,* That the overfeers of the poor of
the feveral townfhips, within every of the
counties within this province, in all future
rates and affeffments to be made for the fupport of the poor in their refpective townfhips,
fhall rate and affefs all perfons according to
their eftates they have in the townfhip, which
fhall not exceed the rates and affeffments made
by the county affeffors refpectively.

Affeff-
ments by
overfeers
not to ex-
ceed the
county af-
feffments.

And Whereas fome doubts have arifen on
the act of affembly paffed in the eighth year
of the prefent reign, intituled, *A fupplement
to the feveral acts of affembly of this province,
for the relief of the poor,* whether indented
healthy fervants, legally imported or brought
into the faid province and coming directly from
Europe, can by the faid act acquire a legal fettlement within the city of Philadelphia, or
within any of the townfhips aforefaid, although they duly ferve therein for the fpace of
one year or upwards within the faid city or
townfhips refpectively, unlefs the mafter or
miftrefs of fuch fervants, or the fervants themfelves fhall give notice in writing to the overfeers of the poor, where they are come to refide: For removing of which doubts, *Be it
enacted*

Servants from Europe acquire a legal settlement in the place where they first serve one year without notice. *enacted by the authority aforesaid,* That all and every such servant or servants so legally and immediately imported or brought from Europe into the city of Philadelphia, or any of the townships aforesaid, and shall duly serve his or her master or mistress for the space of one year; then, and in every such case, every such servant and servants shall, and are hereby declared to acquire a legal settlement in the said city or township where such service is performed, without giving any such notice, as is herein before mentioned, any thing in the act of assembly aforesaid contained to the contrary notwithstanding.

If assigned to a person in another township notice must be given. But if at any time afterwards, during the time for which any such servant is or shall be bound, his or her master or mistress, shall sell or assign over the time of such servant or servants, to any other person or persons dwelling in any other township or place, than that wherein such servant on their first importation into the province aforesaid were bound or assigned over, every such master and mistress, and their servants are hereby declared to be within the meaning of the said act of assembly, and shall give the notice thereby directed, or otherwise shall be liable to the pains and penalties therein contained.

Overseers to keep books for entering notices; such books to be delivered to their successors under penalty, &c. *And be it further enacted by the authority aforesaid,* That the overseers of the poor, within the said city and townships respectively, shall provide and keep books, in which they shall make fair entries of the names of all such persons who, in pursuance of the said act, shall give to them the notices thereby directed; and for each entry so to be made, they shall receive six-pence, and no more; which books, at the times of their going out of the said offices, they shall deliver to such who shall succeed them therein, for the like purposes, under

der

der the penalty of twenty fhillings to every of
the faid overfeers who fhall neglect or refufe
the duty herein enjoined them. The one half
thereof to the ufe of the poor, of the faid
city or townfhips refpectively, and the other
half to him or them who fhall fue for the fame,
before any one of the juftices of the county
in which the offence fhall be committed, to be
recovered with full cofts of fuit.

And whereas by an act entituled, *An act
for emitting thirty thoufand pounds in bills of
credit*, paffed in the fecond year of the prefent reign, one thoufand pounds in the faid
bills was lent to the mayor and commonalty of
the faid city, for purchafing a convenient piece
of ground for building an alms-houfe thereon,
for accommodating the poor of the faid city;
and the faid fum fo lent was to be repaid, and
the bills of credit fo borrowed funk by taxes
to be laid on the inhabitants of the faid city
for that purpofe; *And whereas*, in purfuance
of the faid act, a purchafe was made of William Allen, Efquire, of a piece of ground,
commonly called a fquare, fituate in Philadelphia, containing in length four hundred and
fixty eight feet, and in breadth three hundred
and ninety fix feet, bounded eaftward with
Third-ftreet, fouthward with Pine-ftreet, weft-
ward with Fourth-ftreet, and northward with
Spruce-ftreet, to hold to the mayor and commonalty of the faid city of Philadelphia and
their fucceffors for ever, as by indenture of
leafe and releafe from the faid William Allen
to the faid mayor and commonalty, bearing
date refpectively the ninth and tenth days of
April, 1732, may appear, which indentures
fo made were neverthelefs in truft for the benefit of the inhabitants of the city aforefaid
to build an alms-houfe thereon for the ufe of
the

the poor of the faid city, and to be for fuch other public ufes as the faid inhabitants fhould think fitting. *And whereas* an alms-houfe and other buildings have been erected on the premifes, at the expence of the faid inhabitants, to accommodate the poor of the faid city, and divers parts of the faid fquare yet remain, which might be granted out on a confiderable yearly rent, and the taxes ufually raifed on the faid inhabitants thereby much leffened.

Therefore, be it enacted by the authority Mayor, *aforefaid*, That it fhall and may be lawful &c. empowered to for the mayor, recorder and aldermen, of the let part of city of Philadelphia, or a majority of them, the alms-houfe of which the mayor for the time being fhall fquare on be one, together with the affeffors of the faid ground rent. city, or a majority of them; and they are hereby required, to grant, bargain and fell, for the beft annual rent, that can be had for the fame, but not otherwife, unto any perfon or perfons who fhall be willing to purchafe the fame, and to his, her or their heirs and affigns forever, fuch part and parts of the fquare aforefaid, as to them fhall feem fitting, fo always as not to incommode the alms-houfe and buildings thereunto belonging, or fuch as may hereafter be erected. And referving in every fuch fale the beft annual rent as aforefaid to be made chargeable on the ground to be fold, payable to the overfeers of the poor of the faid city and their fucceffors in the faid truft, for the ufe of the poor of the faid city with covenants therein to be contained, to erect within fome reafonable time a good fubftantial brick, or ftone houfe on the premifes of at leaft two ftories in height.

And be it further enacted by the authority aforefaid, That it fhall and may be lawful to and for the faid overfeers of the poor, and
their

their succeſſors in the said truſt, to collect and
receive the rents of the ground so to be bar-
gained and sold of the perſons to whom the
ſame ſhall be so ſold, and to their heirs, executors, adminiſtrators or aſſigns; and on neglect or refuſal to pay the ſame or any part
thereof, as it ſhall become due, to diſtrain or
bring actions of debt for the rents so in arrear
in any court of record, to be held in the county of Philadelphia, to be recovered with coſts
of ſuit: Which rents and ſums of money,
when received, ſhall from time to time, be applied towards the maintenance, employing and
ſetting to work of the poor of the ſaid city
and leſſening the taxes uſually raiſed for that
purpoſe.

*And be it further enacted by the authority
aforeſaid,* That it ſhall and may be lawful for
the overſeers of the poor of the city of Philadelphia, to appoint one or more fit perſon or
perſons to be collector or collectors of the rates
aforeſaid, who ſhall receive for his or their
trouble and ſervice in collecting the ſame nine
pence in the pound. And for the better collecting of the ſaid tax, and enabling the ſaid
collectors, to perform the duties enjoined by
this act, the ſaid overſeers ſhall apply to the
mayor, recorder or any two aldermen of the
ſaid city, for a warrant under their hands and
ſeals to be annexed to their ſaid duplicates,
requiring them, the ſaid collectors, forthwith
to collect and receive from the perſons aſſeſſed,
the ſeveral ſums in their duplicates reſpectively
mentioned, and thereby authoriſing them, on
the neglect or refuſal of any perſon or perſons
so aſſeſſed, for the ſpace of ten days, to levy
the ſame by diſtreſs and ſale of the delinquents'
goods and chattels, or for want thereof, to im-
priſon their bodies in like manner, as by the

E   act

[margin notes] To be received by the overſeers. Overſeers to appoint, collectors of the poor tax.

act for raifing of county rates and levies is provided in refpect to the affeffments thereby
made ; which faid warrants, they the faid may-
or, recorder or aldermen, are hereby authorifed and required to grant.   And the collector
or collectors to be appointed, fhall from time
to time have the duplicates of the affeffments
fo made, delivered to him or them by the faid
overfeers, directing them the faid collectors to
demand of the parties the refpective fums of
money wherewith they are chargeable; which
faid fums of money the collector or collectors
fhall, fo foon as they receive the fame, immediately pay to the faid overfeers, whofe receipts
fhall be the collectors' fufficient difcharges.

Penalty on And if the faid collectors, or any of them,
collectors fhall refufe or neglect to collect the faid affeff-
not per-
forming ments refpectively, or any part thereof, and
their duty. pay the fame to the overfeers of the poor,
when required thereunto, fo as to complete
and pay in the whole fum in his duplicate in
three months after his receiving the fame,
(fuch deficiencies as the mayor, recorder and
aldermen, of the city aforefaid, fhall allow of,
only deducted) every fuch collector fo refufing
or neglecting, fhall forfeit and pay to the faid
overfeers for the ufe of the poor five pounds,
and fhall alfo pay all the arrearages of fuch
affeffment, which he was appointed to collect;
which fhall be levied by a warrant under the
hand and feal of the mayor for the time being,
or recorder, or any alderman of the faid city,
directed to the fheriff of the county of Philadelphia, who is hereby impowered and obliged to execute fuch warrant upon the goods
and chattels of the party fo offending.   And
in cafe goods and chattels fufficient to make
fatisfaction cannot be found, then to imprifon
fuch offender until payment be made. And every
collector

collector, being fo levied on, and having made
full fatisfaction as aforefaid, is hereby impowered to levy for his own ufe upon all fuch as
fhall refufe or neglect to pay the faid arrearages.

And whereas the employing fuch of the
poor of the city of Philadelphia as are able
to work, but likely otherwife to become
chargeable, as well as employing thofe who
are or may be in the alms-houfe, will be of
great fervice, and help to eafe the inhabitants
of the taxes affeffed for the relief of the poor of
the faid city. And the overfeers of the poor,
from the nature of their office, having the beft
opportunity of being acquainted with the circumftances and abilities of the poor through-
out the faid city, and being frequently at the
alms-houfe, are acquainted with the abilities
and circumftances of the poor therein: *Be it
enacted by the authoity aforefaid*, That the
overfeers of the poor of the city of Philadelphia, or fome fit perfon by them to be appointed, and who fhall be accountable to them
from time to time, fhall have full power and
authority, and are hereby ftrictly enjoined and
required to purchafe junk, hemp, flax, wool,
yarn, worfted or any other proper materials
for employing, and keeping poor perfons to
work and diftribute and give out fuch quanti-
ties thereof as they fee fit, to fuch poor perfons in the faid city, as are likely to become
chargeable for want of employment, and to
employ fuch perfons in manufacturing the fame,
and to make them a reafonable allowance for
their labor.

*And be it further enacted by the authority
aforefaid*, That every perfon hereafter to be
appointed keeper of the alms-houfe, fhall give
bond to the overfeers of the poor of the faid

Overfeers to fet the poor to work.

Keeper of the alms-houfe his duty.

city

city with sufficient securities for the due and faithful execution of his office, and for the care and good management of what shall be committed to his trust; and shall keep just and true accounts of all materials, bedding, goods and other things, brought into the said almshouse, and of the work done there, and shall be accountable to the overseers of the same; any law, usage or custom of this province to the contrary notwithstanding.

And be it further enacted by the authority aforesaid, That all and every the overseers of Overseers atPhiladel-the poor of the city of Philadelphia, shall at phia to account with the mayor, their going out of their office, render a fair and true account to the mayor, recorder and &c. aldermen, at their sessions of the peace in April, yearly, and every year, of all the monies, goods and effects received by them, or which have come to their hands or possession for the use of the poor, and of the produce of the labor of the poor under their care, or who have been employed by them; and how the same hath been applied or disposed of; and also what remains in their hands, and what stock, materials or other things remain in the almshouse, and what stock and materials remain in the hands of the poor out of the alms-house under their employ, and shall pay and deliver the same to the succeeding overseers. And if the said overseers or any of them, shall neglect or refuse to render such account, or to pay and deliver such monies or effects as aforesaid, it shall and may be lawful to and for the mayor, recorder and aldermen, to commit such overseer or overseers to the county goal, until such overseer or overseers shall render a true and fair account, and pay and deliver such monies, goods and effects, as aforesaid; and further, That they, the said overseers of the poor of the

the faid city, fhall be obliged to perform the fame duties, and be fubject to the fame penalties, as by this and former acts of affembly, with regard to the city aforefaid, are directed and inflicted.

And be it further enacted by the authority aforefaid, That fo much of the act entituled, *An act for the relief of the poor;* and other acts of affembly fince made, as are repugnant to the provifions made by this act, are hereby repealed, made null and void; but as to every other part of the fame acts, that they be and remain in full force and virtue as if this act had not been made.

So much of the act for the relief of the poor, and fuch other acts as are repugnant to this repealed.

An act for the better employment, relief and fupport of the poor, within the city of Philadelphia, the diftrict of Southwark, the townfhips of Moyamenfing and Paffyunk and the Northern Liberties.

WHEREAS the poor within the city of Philadelphia, the diftrict of Southwark, the townfhips Moyamenfing & Paffyunk, and the Northern Liberties, are become very burthenfome and expenfive to the inhabitants, and the charge of their fupport is likely to increafe, without affording them fo comfortable a fubfiftance as might otherwife be fupplied, for want of proper buildings, and due regulations for their employment and relief: *And whereas* divers inhabitants of this province are charitably difpofed to contribute largely towards fo good a work, if fuch contributors might be incorporated, with proper powers and privileges for carrying on and compleating the fame, and a fum of money could be raifed by law within the city, diftrict and townfhips aforefaid, and appropriated to the purpofes aforefaid: *Therefore be it enacted*
by

by the honorable JOHN PENN, Efquire,
lieutenant governor, under the honorable
Thomas Penn and Richard Penn, Efquires,
true and abfolute proprietaries of the province
of Pennfylvania, and counties of New-caftle,
Kent and Suffex, upon Delaware, by and with
the advice and confent of the reprefentatives
of the freemen of the faid province, in general affembly met, and by the authority of the
fame, That it fhall and may be lawful to and
for every perfon, who fhall contribute the fum
of ten pounds, or more, towards founding,
providing and eftablifhing a building or buildings, for the reception, employment and relief of the poor of the city of Philadelphia,
diftrict of Southwark, the townfhips of Moyamenfing and Paffyunk, and the Northern Liberties, or as many of the faid contributors
as fhall think fit, to meet on the fecond Monday in the month of May next, and on the
fame day, in the fame month, yearly, for ever,
at fome convenient place in the faid city, then
and there to elect, by ballot, twelve of their
own number to be managers of the faid contributors, and building or buildings, and one
other perfon to be treafurer, until the next
annual election.

Perfons contributing ten pounds to meet yearly and elect twelve managers and a treafurer.

II. *And be it further enacted by the authority
aforefaid,* That the faid contributors fhall for
ever hereafter, in name and in fact, be one
body politic and corporate in law, to all intents
and purpofes whatfoever, and fhall have perpetual fucceffion, and may fue and be fued,
plead or be impleaded, and fhall be incorporated by the name of *Contributors to the relief and employment of the poor, in the city
of Philadelphia,* and by that name fhall and
may receive, take and hold any lands, tenements or hereditaments, not exceeding the
yearly value of one thoufand pounds, and
any

Contributors incorporated.

any goods and chattels whatfoever of the gift,
alienation, bequeft or devife of any perfon or
perfons whatfoever; and are hereby impowered and authorifed to ufe one common feal, in
their bufinefs relating to the faid corporation,
and the fame at their pleafure to change and
alter.

III. And for the better governing and ma-
naging the faid corporation, *Be it further enacted by the authority aforefaid,* That the faid
managers, or any eight of them, fhall, and
they are hereby authorifed, enjoined and required, to meet together on the third Monday
in the month of May, yearly, and at all fuch
other times as they fhall judge neceffary, at
fome convenient place in the faid city, on reafonable notice thereof given to each of them,
to appoint proper officers and fervants for carrying on the bufinefs of the faid corporation,
and to make and ordain, by a majority of votes
all fuch good and wholefome ordinances, rules
and by-laws, as they fhall think convenient
and neceffary for the direction, government
and fupport of the alms-houfe, and houfe of
employment, and the revenues thereto belonging, and alfo for the maintenance and employment of all fuch poor perfons as fhall be tak-
en into or under their care; all which ordinances, rules and by-laws fhall be from time
to time inviolably obferved by all perfons con-
cerned, according to the tenor and effect thereof, provided they be not repugnant to the
laws of England, or of this government, and
fhall be approved of by the fpeaker of the
affembly, chief juftice, and attorney general
of this province for the time being.

IV. *And be it further enacted by the authority aforefaid,* That when the faid contributors
fhall have met, and chofen their managers and
treafurer

Managers to meet yearly on the third Monday in May, &c.

Contributors raising £1500 stock, the mayor, &c. impowered to borrow £2000 for the managers, &c.

treafurer as aforefaid, and fhall have raifed, by their contributions, a ftock of fifteen hundred pounds, for and towards the purpofes aforefaid, and fhall make the fame appear, to the fatisfaction of the mayor, recorder and aldermen of the faid city, or a majority of them, of which the mayor or recorder, for the time being, fhall be one, and of the affeffors of the faid city, or a majority of them, it fhall and may be lawful, and the mayor and commonalty of the city of Philadelphia, in whom, as truftees for the benefit of the inhabitants of the city, the title to the lot and piece of ground, whereon the alms-houfe of the faid city is erected, was vefted, are hereby enjoined and required to borrow, of fuch perfon or perfons as fhall be willing to lend, the fum of two thoufand pounds, and to convey the lot and piece of ground, whereon the alms-houfe of the city of Philadelphia is erected, or any part or parts thereof, together with the buildings thereon, by way of mortgage, and as a fecurity for the payment of the faid fum of money, to fuch perfon or perfons as fhall lend the fame; which fum, fo borrowed, fhall be paid to the treafurer of the faid contributors, to be by their managers applied towards purchafing the lot of ground, and erecting the almshoufe, and houfe of employment, herein after mentioned: And when the faid lot fhall be fo purchafed, and the faid houfes erected, then the faid mayor and commonalty, by and with the advice and confent of the affeffors of the faid city, to be teftified by their, or a majority of their, names fubfcribed, as witneffes to the deed, fhall, and they are hereby enjoined and required to grant, bargain and fell the faid lot of ground, with the buildings thereon erected, to any perfon or perfons who fhall be willing

to

to purchase, and to his, her or their heirs and
affigns forever, for the greateft fum or fums
of money that can be procured for the fame,
and, upon receipt of the faid money, to pay
and difcharge the faid fum fo borrowed, with
the intereft thereof, and to pay the refidue to
the treafurer of the faid contributors, to be,
by the managers aforefaid, applied and appropriated to the purpofes in this act mentioned
and directed.

V. *And whereas* the faid lot of ground, fo
as aforefaid directed to be fold, and the houfes
thereon built, were purchafed and erected
at the expence of the inhabitants of the faid
city, and it is but juft and reafonable that,
when the fame fhall be fold, and the money
arifing from fuch fale fhall be applied to the
joint benefit of the faid city, diftrict and townfhips aforefaid, that the inhabitants of the faid
diftrict and townfhips fhould pay to the faid city, their juft and reafonable proportion thereof, *Be it therefore enacted by the authority
aforefaid,* That when the faid lot of ground
fhall be fold as aforefaid, there fhall be raifed
and levied, within five years next after fuch
fale, over and above the fums of money that
may be neceffary, during that time, for the
relief and fupport of the poor of the faid diftrict and townfhips, by a rate or affeffment to
be laid on all eftates, real and perfonal, within
the faid diftrict and townfhips, by the fame perfons, in the fame manner, and under the fame
penalties, to be recovered as the fums of money to be raifed for the relief of the poor are
or fhall be at that time affeffed, levied and recovered, fo much money as fhall be equal to
one-fourth part of the fum and fums of money for which the faid lot of ground fhall be
fold; and that the faid money, fo to be raifed

*Diftrict &
townfhips
within five
years after
the fale of
the lot and
houfes, to
raife a fum
equal to
one-fourth
part of
what they
fold for.*

F   and

and levied on the diſtrict and townſhips aforeſaid, ſhall be paid to the ſaid treaſurer, and
applied, by the managers aforeſaid, in eaſe of
the inhabitants of the ſaid city, towards the
relief and ſupport of the poor thereof.

VI. *And be it further enacted by the autho-*
rity aforeſaid, That if the money to be raiſed
as aforeſaid by contributions, and the ſale of
the lot of ground aforeſaid, ſhall not be ſufficient to defray the expence of purchaſing the
ground, and erecting the houſes herein before
mentioned, it ſhall and may be lawful to and
for the ſaid managers to borrow, from any
perſon or perſons who ſhall be willing to lend,
any ſum or ſums of money, not exceeding in
the whole the ſum of one thouſand pounds, to
be applied towards purchaſing the ground,
and erecting the houſes aforeſaid; and every
lender ſhall immediately receive a certificate in
writing, under the ſeal of the ſaid corporation,
for the payment of the ſum lent, with the intereſt agreed on, not exceeding ſix per centum
per annum; which certificate ſhall be regiſter-
ed in a book to be kept for that purpoſe, and
the intereſt money thereon ſhall be paid, by
the ſaid corporation, every year.

Contribu-
tions, &c.
not being
ſufficient
the manag-
ers may
borrow a
ſum not
exceeding
£1000.

VII. *And be it further enacted by the au-*
thority aforeſaid, That all and every lender or
lenders, his, her or their executors or adminiſtrators, may aſſign and transfer his, her or
their certificate, with all his, her or their right or
intereſt therein, by an indorſement thereon, to
any other perſon or perſons; and ſuch aſſignee
may, in like manner, aſſign again, and ſo to-
ties quoties; and afterwards it ſhall not be in
the power of the perſon ſo aſſigning to make
void, releaſe or diſcharge the ſaid certificate.

Lenders
may tranf-
fer their
certificates.

VIII. And in order to ſecure to the ſaid lenders the reſpective ſums of money ſo lent, with
the

the interest thereof, *Be it further enacted by the authority aforesaid,* That if the contributions which shall be made and given for the purposes aforesaid, from time to time, shall not be sufficient to satisfy and discharge the sums so borrowed, with the interest thereon accruing, when they become due, such deficiency shall be paid and satisfied by a just and proportionable rate or tax, to be laid, assessed and levied on all the estates, real and personal, within the city, district and townships aforesaid, by the same persons, and under the same penalties, to be recovered in the same manner, and in the same proportions, in the said city, district and townships respectively, as the sums of money to be raised for the relief of the poor are or shall at that time be laid, assessed and levied, and when so levied, shall be paid to the treasurer of the said contributors, to be by the said managers paid in discharge of the said loans; and that the mayor, recorder, and two aldermen of the same city, for the time being, and three justices of the county of Philadelphia, upon such insufficiency appearing to them from the accounts of the said managers, which shall be laid before them for that purpose, shall forthwith certify the same to the overseers of the poor of the said city, district and townships, in writing, under their hands, in order that the said deficiency may be laid, assessed and levied, in manner aforesaid.

Deficiency in contributions to be supplied by tax, &c.

IX. *And be it further enacted by the authority aforesaid,* That the accounts of the disbursements of the money, for which the said lot of ground shall be sold, and of the money to be borrowed on certificate as aforesaid, and of such parts thereof as shall be expended, and of the rents and interest of any real and personal estate given to the said corporation,

Accounts of disbursements to be published annually.

together

together with an account of fuch donations, fhall be fairly drawn out, and publifhed annually in the Pennfylvania Gazette, or other news-paper; and that the faid corporation fhall, at all times when required, fubmit their books, accounts, affairs and œconomy, to the infpection and free examination of fuch vifitors, as fhall be from time to time appointed, by the affembly of this province, to vifit, infpect and examine the fame.

X. *And be it further enacted by the authority aforefaid,* That the faid managers fhall not apply or employ any money, or other eftate, exprefsly given or added to the capital ftock, in any other way than by applying its annual income, intereft or rent, towards the purpofes mentioned in this act.

Managers to apply the intereft only of the capital ftock.

XI. *And be it further enacted by the authority aforefaid,* That the faid managers, as foon as conveniently may be after the publication of this act, fhall, and they are hereby enjoined and required to purchafe a lot or lots of ground, adjoining each other, in the faid city, and to erect thereon a commodious building or buildings, and to appropriate one part thereof, to be called the alms-houfe, to and for the reception and lodging of all fuch of the poor of the faid city, diftrict and townfhips as fhall be incapable of contributing towards their fupport by their labor; and another part or parts thereof to and for the reception, lodging and employment of all fuch of the poor of the places aforefaid, as fhall be able to work; and that the faid managers fhall from time to time receive, provide for and employ, according to the true intent and meaning of this act, all fuch poor, indigent and needy perfons, as fhall be entituled to relief in the faid city, diftrict and townfhips, by

Managers to purchafe lots and erect buildings, &c.

the

the laws of this province, and shall be legally sent there, by an order or warrant for the same, under the hands and seals of any two justices of the peace of the said city, or any two justices of the counties within this province respectively; and for that purpose shall hire servants, and provide all necessary materials and implements; and shall also receive into the said building or buildings all such persons, as shall offer to work, under their care and direction, for their maintenance, at such wages, that their labor will contribute to the advancement of the design of the said corporation.

XII. *And be it further enacted by the authority aforesaid,* That upon complaint made, by any two of the said managers, that any person, from his or her disorderly conduct, gives disturbance to his or her neighbourhood, and is likely to become chargeable to the said city, district or townships, it shall and may be lawful for any two magistrates of the said city, or any two justices of the peace of the county of Philadelphia respectively, if, upon hearing the party, they shall adjudge the complaint to be well founded, to commit such disorderly person, residing within the said city, district or townships aforesaid respectively, to the said house of employment, for any time not exceeding three months, unless he or she shall find security, at the discretion of the magistrates or justices aforesaid, in any sum not exceeding fifty pounds, for his or her good behaviour, and more orderly demeanor, during the space of six months; and also upon complaint, and due proof made, by any two of the said managers, to any magistrates of the said city, that any person under their care, in the said house of employment, hath behaved
and

Disorderly persons to be committed to the house of employment, &c.

and demeaned him or herself in a diforderly manner, or hath refufed or neglected to do and perform his or her daily labor or tafk, or hath refufed or neglected to obey, keep and obferve the ordinances, rules and by-laws of the faid corporation, to order and direct fuch moderate and proper correction to be given to fuch offender, as the nature of the cafe fhall require.

XIII. *And whereas* great numbers of rogues, vagabonds, and other idle and diffolute perfons, frequently come from the neighbouring provinces into the faid city, diftrict and townfhips, and there take up their abode, without following any labor, trade or bufinefs, or having any vifible means of fubfiftence, and are not only dangerous members of fociety, but in the end become burthenfome to the public: *Be it therefore enacted by the authority aforefaid,* That it fhall and may be lawful for any juftice of the peace of the city or county aforefaid, to apprehend, and, upon due examination and proof, commit to the faid houfe of employment, all rogues, vagabonds, and other idle, diffolute and diforderly perfons, found loitering or refiding in the faid city, diftrict or townfhips aforefaid, who follow no labor, trade, occupation or bufinefs, and have no vifible means of fubfiftence, whereby to acquire an honeft livelihood, there to be kept at hard labor, for any term not exceeding three months; and the faid managers are required to receive fuch perfons, and employ them, according to the tenor of fuch commitments.

Rogues, &c. having no vifible means of fubfiftence, to be committed to the houfe of employment, and kept at hard labor.

XIV. *And be it further enacted by the authority aforefaid,* That for and towards the relief, fupport and employment of the poor aforefaid, the overfeers of the poor of the faid city, diftrict and townfhips refpectively, fhall shall pay the monies by them respectively levied and raised, from time to time, for the maintenance, support and employment of their respective poor, to the treasurer of the said corporation, after having deducted thereout the charges which shall arise from the reception or removal of their poor respectively; which said money shall be applied and appropriated to and for the uses aforesaid, by the said managers, and to no other whatever.

Overseers to pay the money by them received to the treasurer of the corporation.

XV. *And be it further enacted by the authority aforesaid,* That the respective treasurers for the time being, before they enter on the execution of their offices, shall become bound to the said corporation, with one or more sufficient sureties, in an obligation of four thousand pounds, conditioned for the true and faithful discharge of their said offices; and that, at the expiration of their said respective offices, they will well and truly pay and deliver over to the succeeding treasurer, all the money, books, accompts, bonds and papers, belonging to the said corporation, which shall then be remaining in their hand, custody and possession.

Treasurers to give bond, &c.

An act for amending the act, entituled, An act for the better employment, relief and support of the poor, within the city of Philadelphia, the district of Southwark, the townships of Moyamensing and Passyunk, and the Northern Liberties.

All the parts of this act but the fifth & sixth sections are obsolete, & therefore not inserted.

Sect. V. *And whereas* great numbers of rogues, vagabonds, and other idle and dissolute persons, frequently come into the said city, district and townships, and there take up their abode, without following any labor, trade or business, or having any visible means of subsistence and are not only dangerous members of society, but in the end become burthensome

Rogues, vagabonds, &c. having no visible means of subsistence, to be committed to the house of employment, and kept at hard labor.

thenfome to the public: *Be it therefore enacted by the authority aforefaid,* That it fhall and
may be lawful for any juftice of the peace of
the city or county aforefaid, to apprehend,
and, upon due examination and proof, commit to the faid houfe of employment all
rogues, vagabonds, and other idle, diffolute
and diforderly perfons, found loitering or refiding in the faid city, diftrict or townfhips
aforefaid, who follow no labor, trade, occupation or bufinefs, and have no vifible means
of fubfiftence, whereby to acquire an honeft
livelihood, there to be kept at hard labor for
any term not exceeding one month; and the
faid managers are required to receive fuch
perfons, and employ them according to the
tenor of fuch commitments.

VI. *And be it further enacted by the au-*
Part of *thority aforefaid,* That fo much of the faid
former acts recited act of affembly, as is hereby altered
repealed. and fupplied, fhall be, and is hereby declared
to be, repealed, null and void, and that the
refidue thereof fhall be, and is hereby declared to be, in full force and virtue to all intents
and purpofes, as if this act had not been
made.

*An act to prevent the mifchiefs arifing from the
encreafe of vagabonds, and other idle and
diforderly perfons within this province.*

WHEREAS the number of rogues,
vagabonds, and other idle and diforderly perfons daily increafes in this province,
to the great lofs and annoyance of the inhabitants thereof, for remedy whereof, *Be it
enacted by* the honorable JOHN PENN, Efquire,
lieutenant governor, under the honorable
Thomas Penn and Richard Penn, Efquires,
true and abfolute proprietaries of the province
of

of Pennsylvania, and counties of New-castle, Kent and Suffex upon Delaware; by and with the advice and confent of the reprefentatives of the freemen of the faid province, in general affembly met, and by the authority of the of the fame, that all perfons who fhall unlawfully return to fuch city, townfhip or place from whence they have been legally removed, by order of two juftices of the peace, without bringing a certificate from the city, townfhip or place to which they belong; and all perfons who, not having wherewith to maintain themfelves and their families, live idly, and without employment, and refufe to work for the ufual and common wages given to other labourers, in the like work in the city, townfhip or place, where they then are, and all perfons going about from door to door, or placing themfelves in ftreets, highways or other roads, to beg or gather alms in the city, townfhip or place where they dwell, and all other perfons wandering abroad and begging; and all perfons who fhall come from the neighbouring colonies, or any of them, into any townfhip or place within this province, and fhall be found loitering or refiding therein, and fhall follow no labor, trade, occupation or bufinefs, and have no vifible means of fubfiftence, and can give no reafonable account of themfelves, or their bufinefs in fuch townfhip or place, fhall be deemed and are hereby declared to be, idle and diforderly perfons, and liable to the penalties hereby impofed; and that it fhall and may be lawful for any juftice of the peace of the county where fuch idle and diforderly perfons fhall be found, to commit fuch offenders (being thereof legally convicted before him, on his own view or by the confeffion of fuch offenders, or by the oath

What fort of perfons to be deemed idle and diforderly.

G or

or affirmation of one or more credible witnefs or witneffes) to the work-houfe of the faid county, if fuch there be, otherwife to the common goal of the county, there to be kept at hard labor, by the keeper of fuch work-houfe or goal, for any time, not exceeding one month.

II. *And be it further enacted by the authority aforefaid,* That if any perfons fhall be found offending in any townfhip or place againft this act, it fhall and may be lawful for any conftable of fuch townfhip or place, and he is hereby enjoined and required, on notice thereof given him by any of the inhabitants thereof, to apprehend and convey, or caufe to be conveyed, fuch perfon fo offending to a juftice of the peace of the county, who fhall examine and try fuch offenders, and on fuch confeffion or proof, fhall commit them to the work-houfe or goal of the county, there to be kept at hard labor, during the term aforefaid; and if any conftable, after fuch notice given as aforefaid, fhall refufe or neglect to ufe his beft endeavours to apprehend and convey fuch offenders before the juftice of the peace aforefaid, being thereof legally convicted before fuch juftice of the peace, every fuch conftable fhall forfeit and pay to the overfeers of the poor of the townfhip or place where fuch offence fhall be committed, to the ufe of the poor thereof, the fum of ten fhillings, to be levied by diftrefs and fale of the offender's goods, by warrant from fuch juftice, and the overplus, if any, after the charge of profecution and of fuch diftrefs fhall be fatisfied, fhall be returned to fuch offender.

Penalty on conftables not apprehending offenders againft this act, &c.

III. *And be it further enacted by the authority aforefaid,* That any perfon or perfons who fhall conceive him, her or themfelves aggrieved, by any act, judgment or determination, of

Perfons aggrieved may appeal.

any

any juftice or juftices of the peace out of feffions, in and concerning the execution of this
act, may appeal to the next general quarter
feffions of the city or county, giving reafonable notice thereof, whofe orders thereupon
fhall be final.

IV. *And be it further enacted by the authority aforefaid,* That upon the prefentment
of any grand jury, at any court of general
quarter feffions of the peace in and for any
county of this province, that there is no work-
houfe, and that it will be for the benefit and
common good of the fame county to erect or
provide fuch houfe, or that the work-houfe
already provided is not fufficient, and requires
repairs, or an alteration or enlargement, then,
if the juftices of the peace, in their feffions,
fhall approve of the fame, the commiffioners
and affeffors of the county aforefaid, if they
unite in judgment with the faid juftices, and
grand jury, fhall have full power and authority to build, erect, add to, or enlarge, one
convenient work-houfe, and to purchafe a lot
or lots for the building fuch houfe on; and,
for defraying the expence, charge and cofts
thereof, fhall lay, affefs and levy, fuch further and other rate or rates, affeffment or affeffments, on all eftates, real and perfonal,
within their county, as fhall or may be fufficient for the purpofes aforefaid, in the fame
manner, and to be collected in the fame manner, by the fame perfons, and under the fame
penalties, as is or are enjoined and directed in
the laying, affeffing, levying and recovering
the county rates, by the act of general affembly of this province, entituled, *An act for
raifing county rates and levies.*

V. *And be it further enacted by the authority aforefaid,* That the faid juftices in their
general

Marginal note: Prefentment being made to the general quarter feffions in any county, of the want of a work-houfe, &c. manner of proceeding thereon.

Juftices in quarter feffions to appoint a keeper of the work-houfe, &c. general quarter feffions fhall, as often as there may be occafion, nominate and appoint fome capable, difcreet and prudent perfon, to be the keeper of fuch work-houfe, who fhall, at the expence of the county, provide, furnifh and fupply fuch fufficient implements, materials and furniture, for keeping, fetting to work, employing and correcting all idle and diforderly perfons, rogues and vagabonds, who fhall be legally committed to the faid houfe, as the faid juftices and commiffioners fhall direct; which faid expence, together with fuch fum of money as fhall be allowed the faid keeper, for his labor and trouble in his faid office, by the juftices and commiffioners aforefaid, fhall be paid out of the county ftock, and fhall be laid, raifed, levied and recovered, in the fame manner as, by the faid recited act, other county rates and levies are enjoined and directed to be laid, levied and recovered; and that all materials fo found and provided, and worked up in the faid houfe, fhall be the property of the county, and fhall be fold by fuch keeper, in fuch manner as the faid juftices and commiffioners fhall direct and appoint; and all the proceeds thereof, after deducting the fum or fums expended in the fupport and victualling fuch perfons fo committed, agreeably to the order and directions of the faid juftices and commiffioners, if any, fhall be paid by fuch keeper unto the county treafurer, there to remain liable to the draughts of the county commiffioners aforefaid, for the payment of the county debts; and that two of the faid juftices, or any fuch two of them as fhall be appointed at the general quarter feffions of the peace, with one or more of the faid commiffioners, fhall, four times, or oftener, if need be, in every year, vifit the faid work-houfe, and examine

into

into the ſtate and management thereof, and report the ſame to the next general quarter ſeſſions aforeſaid, to the intent that if any thing be amiſs, or not properly conducted, the ſame may, by order of the ſaid ſeſſions, and the county commiſſioners aforeſaid, be re-formed and amended.

VI. *Provided always nevertheleſs*, That nothing in this act contained ſhall be deemed, taken or conſtrued, to extend to the appre-hending, trial and commitment of any rogues, vagabonds, or other idle, diſſolute and diſor-derly perſons, found loitering or reſiding in the city of Philadelphia, diſtrict of South-wark, or townſhips of Moyamenſing and Paſ-fyunk, and the Northern Liberties, mention-ed in the act, entituled, *An act for the better employment, relief and ſupport of the poor, within the city of Philadelphia, the diſtrict of Southwark, the townſhips of Moyamenſing and Paſſyunk, and the Northern Liberties*, any thing in this act contained to the contrary there-of in any wiſe notwithſtanding.

Nothing in this act to extend to the commitment of rogues, &c. in the city of Phila-delphia.

An act to amend the act, entituled, An act for the better employment, relief and ſupport of the poor, within the city of Philadelphia, the diſtrict of Southwark, the townſhips of Moyamenſing and Paſſyunk and the Northern Liberties. Obſolete.

An act to enable the managers of the contribu-tions for the relief and employment of the poor, in the city of Philadelphia, to raiſe the ſum of fourteen thouſand pounds in bills of credit, towards diſcharging their debts, and to provide a fund for redeeming and ſinking the ſaid bills. Obſolete.

An

Obſolete. *An act to continue an act, entituled, An act to amend the act, entituled, An act for the better employment, relief and ſupport of the poor within the city of Philadelphia, the diſtrict of Southwark, the townſhips of Moyamenſing and Paſſyunk, and the Northern Liberties.*

An act for the relief of the poor.

[Paſſed March 9. 1771.]

WHEREAS the laws hitherto made for the relief of the poor have not anſwered all the good purpoſes that were expected from them, *Be it therefore enacted by* the honorable JOHN PENN, Eſquire, lieutenant governor, under the honorable Thomas Penn, and Richard Penn, Eſquires, true and abſolute proprietaries of the province of Pennſylvania, and counties of New-caſtle, Kent and Suſſex, upon Delaware, by and with the advice and conſent of the repreſentatives of the freemen of the ſaid province, in general aſſembly met, and by the authority of the

Mayor, recorder, &c. of Philadelphia, and juſtices of the reſpective counties to meet yearly, on the 25th. of March and appoint overſeers, &c.

ſame, That the mayor or recorder of the city of Philadelphia, with the aldermen of the ſaid city, or any two of them, and the juſtices of the peace of the reſpective counties of this province, or any three of them, ſhall, on the twenty-fifth day of March, yearly and every year, unleſs the ſame ſhall happen on a Sunday, and in ſuch caſe on the day following, meet at ſome convenient place within the ſaid city, and in the ſeveral counties reſpectively, and there nominate and appoint twelve ſubſtantial inhabitants of the ſaid city, four of the Northern Liberties, four of the diſtrict of Southwark, and two of every borough and other townſhip within their reſpective juriſdictions,

tions, to be overfeers of the poor of the faid
city, diftrict, boroughs and townfhips; for
which purpofe the overfeers going out of office fhall, on the day aforefaid, return to the
faid magiftrates and juftices, the names of
twelve fubftantial inhabitants, or more, for
the city, four or more for the faid diftrict,
four or more for the faid Liberties, and two
or more for each borough and other townfhip,
out of which number, fucceffors in the faid
office fhall be appointed by the faid magiftrates
and juftices for the enfuing year. And if any
overfeer fhall refufe or neglect to make fuch
return as aforefaid, he fhall forfeit and pay
any fum not exceeding ten pounds. *Provided always*, That the overfeer or overfeers making fuch return fhall give notice thereof, in
writing, at leaft fix days before the twenty-
fifth day of March, to the perfon or perfons,
whofe name or names are fo to be returned,
or leave them at his or their dwelling-houfe or
place of abode. And if any overfeer fhall
die, fail to make a proper return, remove, or
become infolvent, before the expiration of his
office, two of the faid aldermen or juftices refpectively, on due proof being thereof made
before them, may appoint another in his ftead.

II. *And be it further enacted by the authority aforefaid*, That every overfeer fo nominated and appointed fhall, before he enters upon the execution of his office, take an oath
or affirmation refpectively, according to law,
which any alderman in the faid city, or any
juftice in the county refpectively, is hereby
authorifed and impowered to adminifter; *That
he will difcharge the office of overfeer of the
poor truly, faithfully and impartially, to the
beft of his knowledge and ability.*

III. *And be it further enacted by the authority aforefaid*, That it fhall and may be lawful
for

Margin notes: Overfeers going out of office to return the names. Penalty on refufal or neglect. Six days notice to be given to the perfons returned. Overfeers to take an oath or affirmation.

for any two juftices of the peace for the coun-ty, and the mayor or recorder and any two al-dermen of the city of Philadelphia, upon complaint made to them by the managers, elected by the contributors to the relief and employment of the poor in the city of Phila-delphia, or by a majority of them, that a fum of money is wanting, or likely fo to be, to fupport and employ the poor in the houfe of employment in the faid city, to iffue their warrant, under their hands and feals, directed to the overfeers of the poor of the faid city, diftrict of Southwark, and townfhips of Moy-amenfing, Paffyunk, and the Northern Liber-ties, requiring them forthwith to levy, collect and raife, fuch and the fame rate, by a joint affeffment on all eftates, real and perfonal, and taxables, in the manner, and under the fame penalties, within the faid city, diftrict and townfhips, herein after directed for levying, collecting and raifing fuch rates in the feveral boroughs and other townfhips in this province, as to the faid juftices, and mayor or recorder and aldermen, fhall appear neceffary for the

purpofes aforefaid. And if any of the faid overfeers fhall neglect or refufe to levy, col-lect and raife the faid rate, fo ordered by the faid juftices, mayor or recorder and aldermen, and to pay the fame, after the charges arifing from the reception and removal of their re-fpective poor, and of collecting the faid rate, are deducted, to the treafurer of the corpora-tion of contributors to the relief and employ-ment of the poor in the city of Philadelphia, within two months after the receipt of fuch order or warrant, every fuch overfeer, being thereof legally convicted, fhall forfeit to the faid corporation the fum of fifty pounds.

IV. *And be it further enacted by the au-thority aforefaid*, That it fhall and may be law-ful

ful to and for the overfeers of the poor of the
feveral boroughs and townfhips within this
province (the townfhips of Moyamenfing, Paffyunk and the Northern Liberties aforefaid,
only excepted) having firft obtained the approbation of any two juftices of the peace in the
fame county, to make and lay a rate or affeffment, not exceeding three-pence in the pound
at one time, upon the clear yearly value of all
the real and perfonal eftates within the faid
boroughs and townfhips refpectively, and fix
fhillings per head on every freeman, not otherwife rated for his eftate, in every three-penny
tax, and fo in proportion for any leffer rate or
affeffment; which faid affeffments may be repeated, by the authority aforefaid, as often
in one year as fhall be found neceffary for the
fupport of the poor, to be employed in providing proper houfes and places, and a convenient ftock of hemp, flax, thread, and other
ware and ftuff, for fetting to work fuch poor
perfons as apply for relief, and are capable of
working, and alfo for relieving fuch poor, old,
blind, impotent and lame perfons, or other
perfons not able to work, within faid boroughs
and townfhips refpectively, who fhall therewith
be maintained and provided for.

V. *And be it further enacted by the authority aforefaid*, That it fhall and may be lawful
to and for the overfeers of the poor of the
faid boroughs and townfhips, to contract with
any perfon or perfons for a houfe or lodging,
for keeping, maintaining and employing, any
or all fuch poor in faid boroughs and townfhips refpectively, as fhall be adjudged proper
objects of relief, and there to keep, maintain
and employ all fuch poor perfons, and take
the benefit of their work, labor and fervice,
for and towards their maintenance and fupport;

H   and

Side notes:

Overfeers of the poor of the feveral townfhips, &c. with the approbation of two juftices, to lay a rate or affeffment, &c.

The fame to be repeated as often as neceffary in one year, &c.

Overfeers of boroughs to contract for a houfe or lodging for maintaining and employing the poor, &c.

and if any poor perfon fhall refuſe to be lodg-
ed, kept, maintained and employed in ſuch
houſe or houſes, he or ſhe ſhall be put out of
the book, and ſhall not be entituled to receive
relief from the overſeers during ſuch refuſal.

VI. *And be it further enacted by the autho-*
rity aforeſaid, That the overſeers of the ſaid
boroughs and townſhips, in laying the ſaid
rates, ſhall be guided by the county aſſeſſment
on other occaſions, having due regard to every man's eſtate within the borough or townſhip ſo to be rated and aſſeſſed; and ſhall enter ſuch rates fairly in a book, of which a
fair duplicate, ſigned by them, ſhall be delivered to the juſtices, who ſhall allow the ſame,
if they find it juſt and reaſonable, without fee
or reward, and ſhall permit any inhabitant to
inſpect the rates, at all ſeaſonable times, without any fee or reward, and ſhall give copies,
on demand, being paid at the rate of ſix-pence
for every twenty-four names; and if any overſeers ſhall not permit any inhabitant to inſpect,
or ſhall refuſe to give copies as aforeſaid, he
ſhall forfeit twenty ſhillings to the party grieved, to be recovered as debts under forty ſhillings are directed by law to be recovered.

(margin: Overſeers to be guided by the county aſſeſſment in laying their rates, &c.)

VII. *And be it further enacted by the autho-*
rity aforeſaid, That if any perſon or perſons,
ſo rated or aſſeſſed in the ſaid city or diſtrict,
or any borough or townſhip, ſhall refuſe to
pay the ſum or ſums on them charged, it ſhall
and may be lawful to and for the ſaid overſeer
or overſeers (having firſt obtained a warrant,
under the hand and ſeal of any magiſtrate of
the ſaid city, or any juſtice of the peace of
the county reſpectively, where the ſaid aſſeſſment is made, who is hereby impowered to
grant ſuch warrant) to levy the ſame on the
goods and chattels of the perſon or perſons ſo
refuſing;

(margin: Perſons refuſing to pay the ſums rated, the ſame to be levied on their goods and chattels.)

refuſing; and in caſe ſuch perſon ſhall not, within three days next after ſuch diſtreſs made, pay the ſum or ſums on him aſſeſſed, together with the charge of ſuch diſtreſs, that the ſaid overſeer or overſeers may proceed to the ſale of the goods diſtrained, rendering to the owner the overplus, if any, that ſhall remain on ſuch ſale, reaſonable charges being firſt deducted. And in caſe ſuch perſon or perſons have no goods and chattels, whereby they may be diſtrained, it ſhall be lawful for the ſaid juſtices, magiſtrate or juſtice reſpectively, to commit the offenders to priſon, there to remain, without bail or mainprize, until they have paid the ſame. *Provided always*, That if any perſon or perſons ſhall find him, her or themſelves aggrieved with ſuch rate or aſſeſſment, it ſhall be lawful for the magiſtrates or juſtices of the peace, at their next general quarter ſeſſions for the city or county reſpectively, upon petition of the party, to take ſuch order therein, as to them ſhall be thought convenient, and the ſame to conclude and bind all parties; and the overſeers ſhall forbear to proceed in ſuch ſale, till the ſame be determined in the quarter ſeſſions.

Where there are no goods offender to be committed to priſon.

Perſons aggrieved may appeal to quarter ſeſſions.

VIII. *And be it further enacted by the authority aforeſaid*, That it ſhall and may be lawful for the managers of the houſe of employment in the city of Philadelphia, or a majority of them, and the overſeers of the poor of the boroughs and townſhips aforeſaid, by the approbation and conſent of two or more magiſtrates of the ſaid city, or two juſtices of the peace of the county, to put out as apprentices all ſuch poor children, whoſe parents are dead, or ſhall be by the ſaid magiſtrates, or juſtices and managers, found unable to maintain them; males to the age of twenty-one and females to the age of eighteen years.

Managers of the houſe of employment to put out poor children as apprentices

IX. *And*

IX. *And be it further enacted by the authority aforesaid,* That no person or persons shall be admitted or entered in the poor book of the said house of employment, or of any of the said boroughs or townships, or receive relief, before such person or persons shall have procured an order from two magistrates or justices of the peace for the same; and in case the said managers or overseers shall enter in their books, or relieve any such poor person or persons, without such order, they shall forfeit all such money or goods, so paid or distributed, unless such entry and relief shall be approved of by two magistrates or justices as aforesaid.

X. *And be it further enacted by the authority aforesaid,* That the overseers of the city of Philadelphia, the district of Southwark, and the township of the Northern Liberties, Moyamensing and Passyunk, shall, on the twenty-fifth day of March in every year, or within six weeks after, render to the justices of the county of Philadelphia, and to the magistrates of the said city respectively, or to any three of them, the mayor or recorder being one, a just account in writing, fairly entered in a book to be kept for that purpose, and signed by them of all sums by them received, or rated and not received, and of all money paid by such overseers, and of all other things concerning their office, which accounts, when settled, shall be signed by the said justices or magistrates, who shall have full power to allow such parts thereof only, as to them shall seem just and reasonable. And if any such overseer or overseers shall refuse or neglect to make and yield up such accounts within such time or if any overseer or overseers, whose office that year expires, shall refuse or neglect to pay all the monies raised by

assess-

Marginal notes:
No person to be entered in the poor books without an order from two magistrates, &c.

Overseers of the city of Philadelphia to render a just account to the magistrates.

affeffments, which fhall remain in their hands, after deducting the charges of receiving and removing paupers as aforefaid; and alfo all other monies, which fhall remain in their hands, by fines, forfeitures or donations to the treafurer of the faid corporation of contributors, and deliver up the faid books, and every thing in his or their hands, concerning the faid office, to his or their fucceffor or fucceffors, or fhall refufe or neglect to collect and pay to the treafurer all fuch fums of money, as are uncollected on the rate or affeffment, at the expiration of his or their office, which they are hereby enabled to collect by warrant under the hand and feal of any one magiftrate within the faid city, or juftice within the faid county refpectively, within fix weeks after his or their going out of office, it fhall and may be lawful, to and for the faid juftices and magiftrates refpectively, or any three of them, to commit fuch overfeer or overfeers to the common goal, there to remain, without bail or mainprize, till fuch overfeer or overfeers fhall give fuch account, and pay and yield up fuch money, books and other things, as they ought in manner aforefaid.

Penalty on their refufing to render their accounts & pay the monies remaining in their hands &c.

XI. *And be it further enacted by the authority aforefaid*, That the freeholders of every borough and townfhip in this province (except the townfhips, of the Northern Liberties, Moyamenfing and Paffyunk) fhall meet together on the third Saturday in March, yearly and every year, and choofe by tickets in writing, three capable and difcreet freeholders, to fettle and adjuft the accounts of the overfeers of the poor of the refpective boroughs and townfhips for the preceding year, and the perfon who fhall have ferved the office of overfeer fhall, on the faid day, or within fifteen days after, deliver and render to the faid freeholders

Freeholders of every borough & townfhip to meet yearly, on the third Saturday in March and chufe three perfons to adjuft the accounts of the overfeers.

holders a juſt account in writing, entered in a book to be kept for that purpoſe, and ſigned by him, of all ſums by him received, and alſo of all materials that have come to his hands during his office, or that ſhall be in his hands, or in the hands of any of the poor, to be wrought, and of the produce of the labor of the poor under his care and of all money paid by ſuch overſeers, and of all other things concerning his office; which accounts, when ſettled, ſhall be ſigned by the ſaid freeholders, or any two of them, who ſhall have full power to allow Overſeers ſuch parts thereof only, as to them ſhall ap-to make pear juſt and reaſonable. And the ſaid over-fair entries of the ſeers ſhall make fair entries in a book, of the names of names of all the poor within their reſpective all poor. boroughs and townſhips, with the time when each of them become chargeable, and of all certificates delivered to them and by whom, with the times when the ſame were delivered; for which trouble the ſaid freeholders or any two of them, ſhall on ſettling their accounts, make ſuch allowances as they ſhall judge reaſon-Penalty on able. And if any of the ſaid overſeers ſhall their refuſ- ing to ren- refuſe or neglect to make and yield up ſuch der their books and accounts, within the time as afore-books and accounts. ſaid, or if any ſuch whoſe office ſhall expire, ſhall refuſe or neglect to pay over the money, and deliver up the books aforeſaid, and every other thing in his hands concerning his ſaid office, to his ſucceſſors or ſhall refuſe or neglect to collect and pay to ſuch ſucceſſors all ſuch ſums of money, as are uncollected on the rate or aſſeſſment at the expiration of his office (which he is hereby impowered to collect by warrant, to be iſſued under the hand and ſeal of any one juſtice of the peace in and for his reſpective county) within thirty days after his going out of office, it ſhall and may be lawful to and for any juſtice of the peace of the

[63]

the said county to commit such overseer to the common goal, there to remain, without bail or mainprize, till such overseer shall give such accounts, and pay and deliver up such money, books and other things as he ought in manner aforesaid.

XII. *Provided always nevertheless,* That if any person shall think himself aggrieved by the settlement of his account by the said freeholders, he may (having first paid over to his successors the balance found in his hands, if any such there be) appeal to the next county court of quarter sessions, who shall, on the petition of the party, take such order therein, and give such relief, as to them shall appear just and reasonable, and the same shall conclude all parties.

XIII. *And be it further enacted by the authority aforesaid,* That overseers of the poor of the boroughs and townships within the several counties of this province (except as before is excepted) shall, at least five days before the third Saturday in March, yearly and every year, during the continuance of this act, give public notice in writing, by affixing the same in four or more of the most public places in their respective boroughs and townships, of the place where the inhabitants and freeholders of the several boroughs and townships shall meet, to elect the freeholders aforesaid for each and every of the said boroughs and townships, according to the directions of this act; which place, so appointed for the said election, shall be as near the center of the respective boroughs and townships, as conveniently may be.

XIV. *And be it further enacted by the authority aforesaid,* That if any person appointed as overseer of the poor of the city of Philadelphia,

Persons aggrieved may appeal

Overseers of boroughs &c. to give notice of the place where the inhabitants are to meet to choose freeholders

Penalty on overseers refusing to serve.

delphia, fhall refufe or neglect to take upon him
the faid office, he fhall forfeit twenty pounds
to the overfeers of the poor of the faid city,
for the ufe of the poor thereof. And if any
perfon appointed as overfeer of the poor of
any borough, townfhip or place, fhall refufe
or neglect to take upon him the faid office, he
fhall forfeit five pounds to the overfeers of the
poor of the faid borough, townfhip or place,
for the ufe of the poor thereof; and the faid
forfeitures fhall be levied by warrant from any
two juftices of the county, or any two magiftrates of the city of Philadelphia refpectively,
under their hands and feals, on the goods and
chattels of fuch perfon or perfons fo neglecting
or refufing, and fold within three days next after fuch diftrefs made; and if there happen
any overplus upon fale thereof, the fame fhall
be paid to the owner or owners, reafonable
charges being firft deducted; and if fuch perfon or perfons, fo neglecting or refufing as
aforefaid, fhall not have goods or chattels
whereby he or they may be diftrained as aforefaid, that then the faid juftices may commit
the offender or offenders to prifon, there to
remain, without bail or mainprize, till the faid
forfeitures fhall be fully fatisfied and paid. And
if any overfeer fhall remove, he fhall, before
his removal, deliver over to fome other overfeer of the city, borough, townfhip or place,
from which he removes, his accounts as aforefaid, with all affeffments, books, papers, money and other things concerning his office;
and upon the death of any overfeer, his executors or adminiftrators fhall, within forty days
after his deceafe, deliver over all things concerning his office to fome other overfeer as
aforefaid, and fhall pay out of the affets, all
money remaining due, which he received by
virtue

In cafe o the death or removal of any overfeer, all papers, books, &c. to be deli-vered to other over-feers.

virtue of his office, before any of his other debts are paid.

XV. *And be it further enacted by the authority aforesaid,* That all gifts, grants, devises and bequests, hereafter to be made, of any houses, lands, tenements, rents, goods, chattels, sum or sums of money, not exceeding in the whole, including all gifts, grants, devises and bequests heretofore made, the yearly value of five hundred pounds, to the poor of any borough or township within this province, (except the townships as before excepted) or to any other person or persons for their use, by deed, or by the last will and testament of any person or persons, or otherwise howsoever, shall be good and available in law, and shall pass such houses, lands, tenements, rents, goods and chattels, to the overseers of the poor of such borough or township, for the use of their poor respectively.

Gifts, grants, &c. not exceeding the yearly value of £500 to be good, &c.

XVI. *And be it further enacted by the authority aforesaid,* That the said overseers of the poor for the city, boroughs, district and townships aforesaid, for the time being respectively, shall for ever hereafter, in name and in fact, be, and they are hereby declared to be bodies politic and corporate in law, to all intents and purposes, and shall have perpetual succession, and by the name of *Overseers of the poor* of the said city, boroughs, district and townships, may sue and be sued, and plead and be impleaded, in all courts of judicature within this province, and by that name shall and may purchase, take or receive any lands, tenements or hereditaments, goods, chattels, sum or sums of money, not exceeding in the whole, including all gifts, grants, devises and bequests heretofore made, the aforesaid yearly value of five hundred pounds, to and for the

Overseers of the poor for the city and different boroughs incorporated.

I use

ufe and benefit of the poor of the faid city,
or each of the faid boroughs, diftrict or townfhips refpectively, of the gift, alienation or
devife, of any perfon or perfons whomfoever,
to hold to them, the faid overfeers, and their
fucceffors in the faid truft, for the ufe of the
faid poor forever.

XVII. *And be it further enacted by the au-*
What is *thority aforefaid,* That if any perfon, who
deemed a fhall come to inhabit in the faid city of Phila-
legal fettle-
ment in this delphia, or in any borough, townfhip or place
province. in this province, fhall for himfelf, and on his
own account, execute any public office, being
legally placed therein, in the faid city, borough, townfhip or place, during one whole
year; or if any perfon fhall be charged with
and pay his or her fhare towards the public
taxes or levies for the poor of the faid city,
borough, townfhip or place, for two years
fucceffively; or if any perfon fhall really and
bona fide take a leafe of any lands or tenements in the faid city, or in a borough, townfhip or place, of the yearly value of ten
pounds, and fhall dwell in or upon the fame
for one whole year, and pay the faid rent, or
fhall become feized of any freehold eftate, in
any lands or tenements in the faid city, or in
any borough, townfhip or place in this province, and fhall dwell in or upon the fame for
one whole year; or if any unmarried perfon,
not having children or child, fhall be lawfully
bound or hired as a fervant in the faid city, or
any of the boroughs, townfhips or places aforefaid, and fhall continue and abide in fuch fervice during one whole year, or if any perfon
fhall be duly bound an apprentice by indenture,
and fhall inhabit in the faid city, or in any borough, townfhip or place, with his or her
mafter or miftrefs, for one whole year; fuch
perfons,

perfons, in any of thefe cafes, fhall be adjudged and deemed to gain a legal fettlement in the
faid city, borough, townfhip or place refpectively, where fuch perfon fhall fo execute an
office, be charged with and pay taxes, take
fuch leafe, or own any fuch freehold eftate,
and dwell thereon as aforefaid, or, being hired or bound, fhall continue and inhabit in a
place for one whole year as aforefaid.

XVIII. *And be it further enacted by the authority aforefaid*, That every indented fervant, Manner
legally and directly imported from Europe in- of indent-
ed fervants
to this province, fhall obtain a legal fettlement gaining a
in the city, borough, townfhip or place, in legal fettle-
ment, &c.
which fuch fervant fhall firft ferve with his or
her mafter or miftrefs the fpace of fixty days,
and if afterwards fuch fervant fhall duly ferve
in any other place for the fpace of twelve
months, fuch fervant fhall obtain a legal fettlement in the city, borough, townfhip or place,
where fuch fervice was laft performed, either
with his or her firft mafter or miftrefs, or on
an affignment; and all mariners coming into
this province, and every other healthy perfon,
directly coming from Europe into this province,
fhall be legally fettled in the city, borough,
townfhip or place, in which he or fhe fhall
firft fettle and refide for the fpace of twelve
months.

XIX. *And be it further enacted by the authority aforefaid*, That every married woman Legal fet-
fhall be deemed, during coverture, and after tlement of
her hufband's death, to be legally fettled in married
women
the place where he was laft legally fettled; but how deter-
if he fhall have no known legal fettlement, mined.
then fhe fhall be deemed, whether he is living
or dead, to be legally fettled in the place where
fhe was laft legally fettled before her marriage.

XX. *And be it further enacted by the authority aforefaid*, That if any perfon or perfons,

Perfons removing out of the city of Philadelphia to any borough, &c. or from any borough, &c. into the city and producing a certificate, how to be provided for.

fons, after the publication of this act, ſhall come out of the city of Philadelphia, or any borough, townſhip or place, into another borough, townſhip or place, within this province, or ſhall come out of any borough, townſhip or place in this province, into the city of Philadelphia, there to inhabit and reſide, and ſhall at the ſame time procure, bring and deliver unto the overſeers of the poor of the city, borough, townſhip or place, where he or ſhe ſhall come to inhabit, a certificate, under the hands and ſeals of the overſeers of the poor of the city, borough, townſhip or place, from whence he, ſhe or they removed, to be atteſted by two or more credible witneſſes, thereby acknowledging the perſon or perſons mentioned in the ſaid certificate to be an inhabitant or inhabitants, legally ſettled in that city, borough, townſhip or place, every ſuch certificate, having been allowed of and ſubſcribed by one or more juſtices of the peace of the city, or of the county where ſuch borough, townſhip or place doth lie, ſhall oblige the ſaid city, borough, townſhip or place, to provide for the perſons mentioned in the ſaid certificate, together with his or her family, as inhabitants of that place, whenever he, ſhe or they ſhall happen to become chargeable to, or be obliged to aſk relief of the city, borough, townſhip or place, to which ſuch certificate was given, and into which he, ſhe or they were received by virtue of the ſaid certificate, and then, and not before, it ſhall and may be lawful for any ſuch perſon, and his or her children, though born in the city, borough, townſhip or place, and his and her ſervants or apprentices, not having otherwiſe acquired a legal ſettlement, there to be removed, conveyed and ſettled in the city, borough, townſhip or place, from whence ſuch certificate

eate was brought, and the witneffes who at-
teft the execution of the certificate by the
overfeers, or one of the faid witneffes, fhall
make oath or affirmation, according to law,
before the juftices who are to allow the fame,
that fuch witnefs or witneffes did fee the overfeers of the poor, whofe names and feals are
thereunto fubfcribed and fet, feverally fign and
feal the faid certificate; and that the names of
fuch witneffes attefting the faid certificate are
of their own proper hand-writing; which faid
juftices fhall alfo certify that fuch oath or affirmation was made before them; and every
fuch certificate fo allowed, and oath or affirmation of the execution thereof fo certified,
by the faid juftices, fhall be taken and received as evidence, without other proof thereof.
And no perfon fo coming by certificate into
the faid city, or any borough, townfhip or
place, nor an apprentice or fervant to fuch
perfon, fhall be deemed or adjudged, by any
act whatfoever, to have gained a legal fettlement therein, unlefs fuch perfon fhall, after
the date of fuch certificate, execute fome public annual office, being legally placed therein,
in the faid city, borough, townfhip or place.

XXI. *And be it further enacted by the authority aforefaid,* That no perfon whatfoever,
who fhall come into any city, borough, townfhip
or place, without fuch certificate as aforefaid
(mariners and other healthy perfons coming
from Europe as aforefaid, excepted) fhall gain
a legal fettlement therein, unlefs fuch perfon fhall give fecurity, if required, at his or her
coming into the fame, for indemnifying and
difcharging the faid city, borough, townfhip
or place, to be allowed by any one magiftrate
or juftice of the peace refpectively.

*No perfon
coming in-
to any city
without a
certificate
to gain a
fettlement,
unlefs, &c.*

XXII. *And be it further enacted by the authority aforefaid,* That upon complaint being
made

Complaint being made by the overseers of the poor of the said city to any one or more of the magistrates of of the said city, or by the overseers of the poor of any borough, township or place, to one or more of the justices of the peace of of the county, wherein such borough, township or place is situate, it shall and may be lawful to and for any two magistrates of the said city, or any two justices of the said county respectively where any person or persons is or are likely to become chargeable to the said city, borough, township or place, in which he, she or they shall come to inhabit, by their warrant or order directed to the said overseers, to remove and convey such person or persons to the city, borough, township, province or place, where he, she or they was or were last legally settled, unless such person or persons shall give sufficient security to discharge and indemnify the said city, borough, township, or place, to which he, she or they is or are likely to become chargeable as aforesaid.

Provided always, That if any person or persons shall think him, her or themselves aggrieved, by any order of removal made by any of the said justices or magistrates, such person or persons may appeal to the justices of the peace, at their next general quarter sessions of the peace, for the county from whence such poor persons shall be removed, and not elsewhere, which said court shall determine the same; and if there be any defects of form in such order the justices in the said sessions shall cause the same to be rectified and amended, without any costs to the party; and after such amendment, shall proceed to hear the truth and merits of the cause; but no such order of removal shall be proceeded upon, unless reasonable notice be given by the overseers of the city, borough, township or place

place appealing, unto the overfeers of the city, borough, townfhip or place, from which
the removal fhall be, the reafonablenefs of
which notice fhall be determined by the juftices, at the quarter feffions to which the appeal
is made; and if it fhall appear to them, that
reafonable time of notice was not given, then
they fhall adjourn the appeal to the next quarter feffions, and there determine the fame.

XXIV. *And be it further enacted by the
authority aforefaid,* That for the more effectual prevention of vexatious removals and frivolous appeals, the juftices in feffions, upon
any appeal concerning the fettlement of any
poor perfon, or upon any proof before them
there to be made, of notice of any fuch appeal to have been given by the proper officer
to the overfeers of the faid city, or of any borough, townfhip or place (though they did not
afterwards profecute fuch appeal) fhall at the
fame feffions order to the party, in whofe behalf
fuch appeal fhall be determined, or to whom
fuch notice did appear to have been given,
fuch cofts and charges, as by the faid juftices,
in their difcretion, fhall be thought moft reafonable and juft, to be paid by the overfeers,
or any other perfon, againft whom fuch appeal fhall be determined, or by the perfon
that did give fuch notice; and if the perfon
ordered to pay fuch cofts and charges fhall live
out of the jurifdiction of faid court, any juftice where fuch perfon fhall inhabit fhall, on
requeft to him made, and a true copy of the
order for the payment of fuch cofts and charges, certified under the hand of the clerk of
the court, by his warrant, caufe the fame to
be levied by diftrefs; and if no fuch diftrefs
can be had, fhall commit fuch perfon to the
common goal, there to remain, without bail

Method of proceeding in cafe of vexatious removals and frivolous appeals

or

or mainprize, until he pays the said costs and charges. And if the said justices on such appeal shall determine in favor of the appellant, that such poor person was unduly removed, they shall, at the same quarter sessions, order and award to such appellant, so much money as shall appear to the said justices to have been reasonably paid by the city, borough, township or place, on whose behalf such appeal was made, towards the relief of such poor person, between the time of such undue removal, and the determination of such appeal, with the costs aforesaid, the said money so awarded, and the costs, to be recovered in the same manner as costs and charges, awarded against an appellant, are to be recovered by virtue of this act as aforesaid.

XXV. *And be it further enacted by the authority aforesaid,* That if any house-keeper or inhabitant of this province shall, after the publication of this act, take into, receive or entertain in his or her house or houses, any person or persons whatsoever (all mariners coming into this province, and every other healthy person coming from Europe immediately into the said province, only excepted) not being persons who have gained a legal settlement in some city, borough, township or place within this province, and shall not give notice in writing, which they are hereby required to do, within three days next after the taking into or entertaining any person or persons in his or her house, within the city of Philadelphia, to the overseers of the poor of the said city, and within ten days next after taking into or entertaining any person or persons in his or her house, in any borough, township or place within this province, to the overseers of the poor of the borough, township

Penalty on house-keepers entertaining persons not having a legal settlement.

ship

ſhip or place where ſuch perſon dwells, ſuch
inhabitant or houſe-keeper, being thereof legally convicted, by teſtimony of one credible
witneſs, on oath or affirmation, before any
one magiſtrate of the ſaid city of Philadelphia,
or before any one juſtice of the peace of the
county where ſuch perſon dwells, ſhall forfeit
and pay the ſum of twenty ſhillings for every
offence; the one moiety for the uſe of the poor
of the ſaid city, borough, townſhip or place reſpectively, and the other moiety to the informer, to be levied on the goods and chattels of
the delinquents, in the manner herein after directed; and for want of ſufficient diſtreſs, the
offender to be committed to the work-houſe of
the ſaid city or county, there to remain, without bail or mainprize, for the ſpace of ten
days. And moreover, in caſe the perſon or
perſons ſo entertained or concealed ſhall become poor, and unable to maintain him or her-
ſelf, and cannot be removed to the place of
his or her laſt legal ſettlement in any other
province, if any ſuch he or ſhe hath, or ſhall
happen to die, and not have wherewithal to
defray the charges of his or her funeral, then,
and in ſuch caſe, the houſe-keeper or perſon
convicted of entertaining or concealing ſuch
poor perſon, againſt the tenor of this act, ſhall
be obliged to provide for and maintain ſuch
poor and indigent perſon or perſons; and in
caſe of ſuch poor perſon's death ſhall pay the
overſeers of the poor ſo much money, as ſhall
be expended on the burying of ſuch poor and
indigent perſon or perſons; and upon refuſal
ſo to do, it ſhall be lawful for the overſeers of
the poor of the ſaid city, borough, townſhip
or place reſpectively, and they are hereby required to aſſeſs a ſum of money on the perſon
or perſons ſo convicted, from time to time, by

a week-

a weekly affeffment, for maintaining fuch poor
and indigent perfon or perfons, or affefs a fum
of money for defraying the charges of fuch
poor perfon's funeral, as the cafe may be;
and in cafe the party convicted fhall refufe to
pay the fum of money, fo affeffed or charged,
to the overfeers of the poor, for the ufes aforefaid, the fame fhall be levied on the goods and
chattels of the offender, in the manner herein
after directed; but if fuch perfons, fo convicted, have no goods or chattels to fatisfy
the money fo affeffed for him or her to pay,
that then it fhall and may be lawful for the
faid magiftrates or juftices to commit the offender to prifon, there to remain, without bail
or mainprize, until he or fhe hath paid the
fame, or until he or fhe fhall be difcharged by
due order of law.

XXVI. *And be it further enacted by the au-*
rity aforefaid, That if any perfon be removed
by virtue of this act, from one county, city,
borough, townfhip or place to another, by
warrant or order, under the hands and feals
of two juftices of the peace, or magiftrates
as aforefaid, the overfeers of the poor of the
city, borough, townfhip or place, to which
the faid perfon fhall be fo removed, are hereby required to receive the faid perfon; and if
any of the faid overfeers fhall refufe or neglect
fo to do, he or they fo offending, upon proof
thereof by one or more credible witneffes, upon oath or affirmation, before any one of the
magiftrates or juftices of the peace of the city
or county where the offender doth refide, fhall
forfeit and pay, for every fuch offence, the
fum of five pounds, to the ufe of the poor of
the city, borough, townfhip or place, from
which fuch perfon was removed, to be levied
by diftrefs and fale of the offender's goods by
warrant,

(marginal note) Penalty on overfeers not receiv-ing perfons removed by warrant

warrant, under the hand and feal of the faid magiftrate or juftice of the peace, which he is hereby required and impowered to make, directed to the conftable of the city, borough, townfhip or place where fuch offender or offenders dwell, returning the overplus, if any be, to the owner or owners, and for want of fufficient diftrefs, then the offender to be committed to the goal of the county where he dwells, there to remain, without bail or mainprize, for the fpace of forty days.

XXVII. *And whereas* it often happens, that poor perfons, fometimes with certificate, and fometimes without, come from the city of Philadelphia into fome townfhip or place within this province, and from fome place or townfhip of this province, into the faid city of Philadelphia, or into fome other townfhip of this province, and conceal themfelves until they become fick or lame, and cannot be removed, or die before they can be removed, by reafon whereof the inhabitants of the city, borough, townfhip or place, where fuch poor perfon or perfons fell fick or died, are put to charges, without any means to relieve themfelves from the payment of the monies expended for the maintenance or burying of fuch poor perfon or perfons, *Be it therefore enacted by the authority aforefaid,* That if any poor perfon or perfons, fhall come out of the city of Philadelphia into any borough, townfhip or place, within this province, or fhall come out of any borough, townfhip or place within the province into the city of Philadelphia, or any other townfhip or place within this province, and fhall happen to fall fick, or die, before he or fhe have gained a legal fettlement in the city, borough, townfhip or place, to which he or fhe fhall come, fo that fuch perfon or perfons

Poor perfons coming from the city of Philadelphia, into any borough, &c. or from thence into the city, and fall fick or die, overfeers to give notice to thofe where fuch perfons laft had a legal fettlement.

fons

fons cannot be removed, the overfeers of the poor of the city, borough, townfhip or place, into which fuch perfon or perfons is or are come, or one of them, fhall, as foon as conveniently may be, give notice to the overfeers of the poor of the city, borough, townfhip or place where fuch perfon or perfons had laft gained a legal fettlement, or to one of them, of the name, circumftances and condition of fuch perfon or perfons; and if the overfeers of the poor, to whom fuch notice

Mode of proceeding in cafe they refufe to re-imburfe the expences. fhall be given, fhall negleft or refufe to pay the monies expended for the ufe of fuch poor perfon or perfons and to take order for relieving and maintaining fuch poor perfon or perfons, or in cafe of his, her or their death, before notice can be given as aforefaid, fhall, on requeft being made, negleft or refufe to pay the monies expended in maintaining and burying fuch poor perfon or perfons, then, and every fuch cafe, it fhall be lawful for any two juftices of the peace of the city or county where fuch poor perfon or perfons where laft legally fettled, and they are hereby authorifed and required upon complaint made to them, to caufe all fuch fums of money, as were neceffarily expended for the maintenance of fuch poor perfon or perfons, during the whole time of his, her or their ficknefs, and in cafe he, fhe or they die, for his, her or their burial, by warrant under their hands and feals, to be directed to fome conftable of the city or county refpectively, to be levied by diftrefs and fale of the goods and chattels of the faid overfeer or overfeers of the poor fo neglecting or refufing, to be paid to the overfeer or overfeers of the city, borough, townfhip or place, where fuch poor perfon or perfons happened to be fick, or to die as aforefaid, said, and the overplus of the monies arising by sale of such goods, remaining in the constable's hands, after the sum of money ordered to be paid, together with the costs of distress, are satisfied, shall be restored to the owner or owners of the said goods.

XXVIII. *Provided always,* That if any of the said overseers, shall think him or themselves aggrieved by any sentence of such justices, or by their refusal to make any order, as is aforesaid, he or they may appeal to the justices of the peace, at their next court of quarter sessions for the county where such justices reside, and not elsewhere; who are hereby authorised and required to hear, and finally to determine the same.

Overseers aggrieved may appeal

XXIX. *And be it further enacted by the authority aforesaid,* That the father and grand father, and the mother and grand mother, and the children of every poor, old, blind, lame and impotent person, or other poor person, not able to work, being of sufficient ability, shall at their own charges relieve and maintain every such poor person, as the magistrates, or the justices of the peace, at their next general quarter sessions, for the city or county where such poor persons reside, shall order and direct, on pain of forfeiting forty shillings for every month they shall fail therein.

Father and grand-father, &c. of poor, impotent persons, being of sufficient ability, to maintain them, &c.

XXX. *And whereas* it sometimes happens that men separate themselves, without reasonable cause, from their wives, and desert their children; and women also desert their children, leaving them a charge upon the said city, or upon some borough, township or place aforesaid, although such persons may have estates, which should contribute to the maintenance of such wives or children, *Be it therefore enacted by the authority aforesaid,* That it shall and

Mode of proceeding in case father or mother desert their children and leave them chargeable.

may

may be lawful for the overfeers of the poor
of the faid city, having firft obtained a warrant or order from two magiftrates of the faid
city; or for the overfeers of any borough,
townfhip or place, where fuch wife or children
fhall be fo left, or where fuch wife or children
fhall be fo neglected, having firft obtained a
warrant or order of any two juftices of the
peace of the county, to take and feize fo much
of the goods and chattels, and receive fo much
of the annual rents and profits of the lands
and tenements of fuch hufband, father or mother, as fuch two magiftrates or juftices fhall
order and direct, for providing for fuch wife,
and for maintaining and bringing up fuch child
or children; which warrant or order being
confirmed at the next quarter feffions for the
city or county refpectively, it fhall and may be
lawful for the juftices there to make an order,
for the overfeers to difpofe of fuch goods and
chattels, by fale or otherwife, or fo much of
them, for the purpofes aforefaid, as the court
fhall think fit, and to receive the rents and
profits, or fo much of them as fhall be ordered by the faid feffions, of his or her lands and
tenements, for the purpofes aforefaid; and if
no eftate, real or perfonal, of fuch hufband,
father or mother, can be found, wherewith
provifion may be made as aforefaid, it fhall
and may be lawful to and for the faid juftices,
in their court of quarter feffions for the city
or county refpectively, to order the payment
of fuch fums as they fhall think reafonable, for
the maintenance of any wife or children fo
neglected, and commit fuch hufband, father
and mother to the common goal, there to remain, until he or fhe comply with the faid order, give fecurity for the performance thereof, or be otherwife difcharged by the faid juftices;

tices; and on complaint made to any magiftrate of the city of Philadelphia, or to any
juftice of the peace in any county, of any wife
or children being fo neglected, fuch magiftrate
or juftice fhall take fecurity from the hufband,
father or mother, neglecting as aforefaid, for
his or her appearance at the next general quarter feffions, there to abide the determination
of the faid court, and for want of fecurity, to
commit fuch perfons.

XXXI. *And be it further enacted by the authority aforefaid*, That the feveral fines, forfeitures and penalties, fum and fums of money,
impofed or directed to be paid by this act, and
not herein otherwife directed to be recovered,
the fame, and every of them, fhall be levied
and recovered by diftrefs and fale of the goods
and chattels of the delinquent or offender, by
warrant, under the hands and feals of one or
more of the aldermen of the city of Philadelphia, for the faid city, and under the hand
and feal of any one juftice of the county, where
the delinquent or offender dwells, or is to be
found; and after fatisfaction made of the refpective forfeitures, fines, penalties and fums
of money, directed to be levied by fuch warrant as aforefaid, together with fuch legal
charges as fhall become due on the recovery
thereof, the overplus, if any, to be returned
to the owner or owners of fuch goods and
chattels, his or her executors or adminiftrators.

XXXII. *Provided always*, That if any perfon or perfons fhall find him or themfelves aggrieved with any judgment of the juftices, giv-
en out of their feffions, in purfuance of this
act, fuch perfon or perfons may appeal to the
next general quarter feffions of the peace, for
the county or city where fentence was given
(except in cafes of removals, and cafes of poor
perfons

Mode of recovering fines, &c.

Perfons aggrieved may ap-peal.

persons becoming chargeable in one place, who are legally settled in another, as is otherwise provided for by this act) whose decision, in all such cases, shall be conclusive.

XXXIII. *And be it further enacted by the* *authority aforesaid,* That if any action shall be brought against any overseer, or other person, who, in his aid, and by his command, shall do any thing concerning his office, he may plead the general issue, and give this act, and any special matter in evidence; and if the plaintiff shall fail in his action, discontinue the same, or become non-suit, he shall pay double costs.

Marginal note: Overseers, &c. sued for any thing done by the directions of this act, may plead the general issue.

XXXIV. *And be it further enacted by the* *authority aforesaid,* That an act of the general assembly of this province, entituled, *An act* *for the relief of the poor;* and another act, entituled, *An act for supplying some defects in* *the law for the relief of the poor;* and another act, entituled, *A supplement to the seve-* *ral acts of assembly of this province for the re-* *lief of the poor;* and another act, entituled, *An act for amending the laws relating to the* *poor;* be and are hereby repealed, annulled, and made void.

Marginal note: Former laws relating to the poor repealed.

XXXV. *Provided always, and be it fur-* *ther enacted by the authority aforesaid,* That nothing in this act contained shall be deemed or construed to extend to abridge, alter or change the powers and duties of the present respective overseers of the poor in any city, borough, township or place, within this province; but that they, the said overseers of the poor, shall continue to hold, exercise, do and perform the respective duties to their offices belonging, until the twenty-fifth day of March next, as fully and amply, to all intents and purposes, as if this act had not been made, any

Marginal note: Nothing in this act to abridge the powers of the overseers till the 25th of March next.

any thing herein contained to the contrary notwithſtanding.

XXXVI. *And be it further enaƈted,* That
ſo much of the aƈt of aſſembly, paſſed in the
ſixth year of his preſent majeſty's reign, entituled, *An aƈt for the better employment, relief
and ſupport of the poor, within the city of
Philadelphia, the diſtriƈt of Southwark, the
townſhips of Moyamenſing and Paſſyunk, and
the Northern Liberties,* as relates to the applying the monies, which ſhall be raiſed in
the ſaid city, diſtriƈt and townſhips, for the
maintenance, ſupport and employment of their
reſpeƈtive poor, or is otherwiſe hereby altered
or ſupplied, ſhall be and is hereby declared to
be repealed, null and void.

XXXVII. *And be it further enaƈted by the
authority aforeſaid,* That this aƈt ſhall continue in force for the ſpace of five years, and
from thence to the end of the next ſitting of
aſſembly, and no longer.

Part of the aƈt of the 6th. of George III. repealed.

Limitation.

[*N. B.* This aƈt by its own limitation expired five
years after it was paſſed, but was revived by an aƈt,
entituled, *An aƈt to revive and put in force the aƈt of general aſſembly of the province of Pennſylvania,* entituled,
*An aƈt for the relief of the poor, and for other purpoſes
therein mentioned.*]

*An aƈt for the better relief of the poor of the
city of Philadelphia, the diſtriƈt of Southwark, and the townſhips of Moyamenſing,
Paſſyunk and the Northern Liberties, in the
county of Philadelphia.*

Obſolete.

*A ſupplement to an aƈt, entituled, An aƈt for
the relief of the poor.*

Obſolete.

L
An

*An act to amend an act, entituled, An act for
the better employment of the poor of the city
of Philadelphia, the district of Southwark,
the townships of Moyamensing, Passyunk
and the Northern Liberties, and to revive and
perpetuate an act, entituled, An act for the
relief of the poor, and for repealing two
other acts herein mentioned.*

Sect. I. WHEREAS the poor within
the city of Philadelphia, the
district of Southwark, and townships of Moyamensing, and the Northern Liberties, have
become very burthenfome, and expensive to
the inhabitants, and the expence thereof is
like to increase: *And whereas*, for remedy
thereof, by employing the faid poor, an act
of affembly was paffed on the eighth day of
February, in the year one thousand seven hundred and fixty-fix, in the late province of Pennfylvania, entituled, *An act for the better employment of the poor of the city of Philadelphia,
the district of Southwark, the townships of
Moyamensing, Passyunk and the Northern Liberties*, whereby all perfons, who should contribute the fum of ten pounds or more, were
incorporated by the name of *Contributors to
the relief and employment of the poor in the
city of Philadelphia*, and fuch of the faid contributors as fhould think fit, where enabled to
meet on the fecond Monday in the month of
May, then next following, and on the fecond
Monday in the month of May, yearly, forever,
at fome convenient place in the faid city, and
then and there to choofe twelve perfons of their
own number to be managers of the faid contributions, and of the buildings to be erected for
the reception, employment and relief of the
poor of the faid city, district and townships, in
purfuance of the faid act.

Sect. II. *And whereas* by the deceafe of
many of the contributors, and the legal difa-
bility of others of the faid contributors who
yet furvive, the choofing of the managers,
and the burthen of ferving in that office, has
devolved upon a fmall number of perfons and
it is now become difficult to procure a fucceffion of managers to fuperintend the alms-houfe
and the houfe of employment in the faid city,
and to provide for, employ and relieve the
poor aforefaid, out of the faid furviving contributors, who are qualified to elect or to be
elected as aforefaid: For remedy whereof, *Be
it enacted by the reprefentatives of the freemen
of the commonwealth of Pennfylvania, in general affembly met, and by the authority of the
fame,* That in cafe the contributors aforefaid
fhall not meet on the fecond Monday in May
next, or in any fucceeding year, in the faid
city, and choofe twelve managers as aforefaid,
or if the faid contributors fhall meet on the fecond Monday in May next, or in any future
year, and having made fuch choice of managers as aforefaid, the perfons then and there
chofen, or a majority of them, fhall not meet
together on the third Monday of the fame
month, in the faid city, as by the faid act
they were directed and enjoined, then, and in
fuch cafe, and upon fuch neglect, whether in
the month of May next, or in the month of
May in any future year, the overfeers of the
poor of the faid city of Philadelphia, diftrict
of Southwark, and townfhips of Moyamenfing and the Northern Liberties, for the time
being, fhall become invefted with all and fin-
gular the powers, authorities, rights, claims,
demands, interefts and eftate, real, perfonal
and mixed, which then fhall be of the faid
corporation, in as ample a manner, and for
the

Corporation of contributors neglecting to meet annually and choofe 12 managers, overfeers to be invefted with their powers.

the fame ufe and purpofes, as the fame are or were invefted in, or ought to be exercifed, poffeffed or enjoyed by the faid corporation.

Sect. III. *And be it further enacted by the au-* thority aforefaid, That the faid overfeers of the poor for the time being, whenever the fucceffion of the faid managers fhall fail as aforefaid, fhall become a body politic and corporate in law, for the purpofe of fuperintending the the houfe of employment, and the other purpofes, for which the faid managers were appointed and conftituted as aforefaid, by the name of *The guardians of the poor in the city of Philadelphia,* with all the powers and faculties of the body politic and corporate; and the faid guardians of the poor in the city of Philadelphia may hold real eftates, no exceeding the yearly value of two thoufand pounds, and may take and receive any grant, gift, bequeft, or alienation of goods and chattels whatfoever.

Incorporated.

Name of the corporation.

Sect. IV. *And be it further enacted by the authority aforefaid,* That the faid eventual corporation of the guardians of the poor in the city of Philadelphia, fhall, half yearly, appoint fix of their number to fuperintend the almshoufe and houfe of employment, to exercife and perform all the authorities of the prefent managers of the faid inftitution, and the faid fix overfeers, fhall, during their continuation as managers as aforefaid, be exempted from all other duties of the faid office of overfeers, and the whole duties thereof fhall be performed by the reft of the faid overfeers.

To appoint fix of their number to fuperintend the alms-houfe.

Sect. V. *And be it further enacted by the authority aforefaid,* That from and after the paffing of this act, any overfeer of the poor of the faid city, diftrict and townfhips, may with the confent of any one juftice of the peace,

Overfeers may afford relief not exceeding £3.

peace, afford relief to the fudden neceffity of any poor perfon, not exceeding the value of three pounds within three months.

Sect. VI. *And be it further enacted by the authority aforefaid,* That one half of the over-feers of the poor, who fhall be nominated and fhall take upon themfelves the duties of the faid office within the faid city, diftrict and townfhips, on the twenty-fifth day of March next, or afterwards, as immediate fucceffors of the prefent overfeers of the poor of the faid city, diftrict and townfhips, fhall not continue in office longer that fix kalender months, and the other half of the faid overfeers fhall continue in office, until the twenty-fifth day of March, one thoufand feven hundred and eighty-three, and that on the twenty-fifth day of September next, or within ten days after, the juftices of the peace of the city and county of Philadelphia, or any three or more of them, fhall meet at the county court-houfe in the faid city, and then and there appoint and conftitute fucceffors to ferve for one year, in the ftead of thofe who fhall be appointed as aforefaid, for fix months; and fo every twenty-fifth day of March, and every twenty-fifth day of September, yearly, for and during the continuance of the act, entituled, *An act for the relief of the poor,* the faid juftices fhall meet at the faid court-houfe, and fhall then and there appoint and conftitute one half of the faid overfeers half yearly, in order that there may be always fome experienced perfons in office. And if any perfon who fhall be appointed an overfeer of the poor, in purfuance of this act, fhall refufe or neglect to ferve in the faid office, he fhall be fined in like fum and the faid fine fhall be levied in like manner, and go to

the

Marginal note: One half of the over-feers not to continue in office longer than fix months and fucceffors to be appointed half yearly.

the fame ufes, as if fuch perfon had been appointed on the twenty-fifth day of March, and
had refufed or neglected to ferve thereupon.

Preamble.   Sect. VII. *And whereas* divers diforderly
perfons by their own lewdnefs, drunkennefs
or other evil practices, have fallen fick, and
become chargeable to the faid city, diftrict
and townfhips, and have been unwilling or
unable to reimburfe the expences, which have
been incurred, in order to their cure and recovery; and it may be fome relief of the inhabitants of the faid city, diftrict and townfhips, who have been put to great charge by
fuch diforderly perfons, and may deter fuch
diforderly perfons, from returning to their
former evil practices, if fuch diforderly perfons where hereafter obliged to make compen-
fation by fervitude.

    Sect. VIII. *Be it therefore enacted by the au-*
Overfeers *thority aforefaid,* That from and after the paf-
with the fing of this act, the overfeers of the poor, of
approbati-
on of two the faid city, diftrict and townfhips, or any
juftices
may bind two of them, with the approbation and con-
out difor- currence of any two juftices of the peace of
derly per-
fons, &c. the city and county of Philadelphia, fhall, and
they are hereby authorifed to bind out, by
indenture or deed-poll, any fuch diforderly
perfons to any mafters or miftrefs and his and
her affigns, who will advance and pay fuch
confideration for fuch fervice as the faid overfeers fhall think fit to accept for the fame;
Provided always, That no married man or
woman, nor any perfon of the age of forty
years, and upwards fhall be liable to be bound
by indenture or deed-poll as aforefaid, and
that no fuch binding fhall be for a longer term
than will be fufficient to reimburfe the overfeers aforefaid the expences incurred in behalf,
and

and on account of such person, and so as the same do not exceed in the whole the space of three years.

Sect. IX. *And whereas* the act, entituled, *An act for the relief of the poor*, passed the ninth day of March, in the year one thousand seven hundred and seventy-one, hath been found by experience to be of great public utility.

Preamble.

Sect. X. *Be it further enacted by the authority aforesaid*, That the said act and every article, clause, matter and thing therein contained, is hereby revived, re-enacted and made perpetual, except the clause limiting the continuance thereof, and such other parts thereof, as are hereby altered, amended and supplied, or relate to the mayor, recorder and aldermen of the city of Philadelphia, whose authority, jurisdiction and power, granted by the said act, shall be exercised by the justices of the peace of the said city, or any three of them, agreeably to the directions of the act, passed the fourteenth day of March, in the year one thousand seven hundred and seventy-seven.

Act past in 1771, made perpetual, except, &c.

Sect. XI. *And be it further enacted by the authority aforesaid*, That an act, entituled, *An act for the better relief of the poor of the city of Philadelphia, the district of Southwark, and the townships of Moyamensing, Passyunk and the Northern Liberties, in the county of Philadelphia*, passed the second day of April, in the year one thousand seven hundred and seventy-nine, and also an act, entituled, *An act for the relief of the poor*, passed the twenty-seventh day of November, in the year one thousand seven hundred and seventy-nine, are hereby repealed and made void.

Former acts repealed.

Sect.

Part of a
former act
repealed.
Sect. XII. *And be it further enacted by the authority aforesaid,* That so much of the act, entituled, *An act for the better employment of the poor of the city of Philadelphia, the district of Southwark, the townships of Moyamensing, Passyunk and Northern Liberties,* passed the eighth day of February, one thousand seven hundred and sixty-six, as incorporates the township of Passyunk with the city of Philadelphia, the district of Southwark, and the townships of Moyamensing and Northern Liberties is hereby repealed and made void.

INDEX.

I N D E X.

*[Where an Afterifm (*) is annexed to a page in this index, the law,
title, or fection to which it refers, is repealed, expired, &c.*

M   Collector,

Work,

W.

F   I   N   I   S.

POVERTY, U. S. A.

THE HISTORICAL RECORD

An Arno Press/New York Times Collection

Adams, Grace. **Workers on Relief.** 1939.

The Almshouse Experience: Collected Reports. 1821-1827.

Armstrong, Louise V. **We Too Are The People.** 1938.

Bloodworth, Jessie A. and Elizabeth J. Greenwood.
The Personal Side. 1939.

Brunner, Edmund de S. and Irving Lorge.
**Rural Trends in Depression Years: A Survey of
Village-Centered Agricultural Communities, 1930-1936.**
1937.

Calkins, Raymond.
**Substitutes for the Saloon: An Investigation Originally
made for The Committee of Fifty.** 1919.

Cavan, Ruth Shonle and Katherine Howland Ranck.
**The Family and the Depression: A Study of
One Hundred Chicago Families.** 1938.

Chapin, Robert Coit.
**The Standard of Living Among Workingmen's Families
in New York City.** 1909.

**The Charitable Impulse in Eighteenth Century America:
Collected Papers.** 1711-1797.

Children's Aid Society.
Children's Aid Society Annual Reports, 1-10.
February 1854-February 1863.

Conference on the Care of Dependent Children.
**Proceedings of the Conference on the Care
of Dependent Children.** 1909.

Conyngton, Mary.
How to Help: A Manual of Practical Charity. 1909.

Devine, Edward T. **Misery and its Causes.** 1909.

Devine, Edward T. **Principles of Relief.** 1904.

Dix, Dorothea L.
On Behalf of the Insane Poor: Selected Reports. 1843-1852.

Douglas, Paul H.
**Social Security in the United States: An Analysis and
Appraisal of the Federal Social Security Act.** 1936.

Farm Tenancy: Black and White. Two Reports. 1935, 1937.

Feder, Leah Hannah.
**Unemployment Relief in Periods of Depression:
A Study of Measures Adopted in Certain American
Cities, 1857 through 1922.** 1936.

Folks, Homer.
**The Care of Destitute, Neglected, and
Delinquent Children.** 1900.

Guardians of the Poor.
**A Compilation of the Poor Laws of the State of
Pennsylvania from the Year 1700 to 1788, Inclusive.** 1788.

Hart, Hastings, H.
Preventive Treatment of Neglected Children.
(Correction and Prevention, Vol. 4) 1910.

Herring, Harriet L.
**Welfare Work in Mill Villages: The Story of Extra-Mill
Activities in North Carolina.** 1929.

The Jacksonians on the Poor: Collected Pamphlets.
1822-1844.

Karpf, Maurice J.
Jewish Community Organization in the United States.
1938.

Kellor, Frances A.
Out of Work: A Study of Unemployment. 1915.

Kirkpatrick, Ellis Lore.
The Farmer's Standard of Living. 1929.

Komarovsky, Mirra.
The Unemployed Man and His Family: The Effect of Unemployment Upon the Status of the Man in Fifty-Nine Families. 1940.

Leupp, Francis E. **The Indian and His Problem.** 1910.

Lowell, Josephine Shaw.
Public Relief and Private Charity. 1884.

More, Louise Bolard.
Wage Earners' Budgets: A Study of Standards and Cost of Living in New York City. 1907.

New York Association for Improving the Condition of the Poor.
AICP First Annual Reports Investigating Poverty.
1845-1853.

O'Grady, John.
Catholic Charities in the United States: History and Problems. 1930.

Raper, Arthur F.
Preface to Peasantry: A Tale of Two Black Belt Counties.
1936.

Raper, Arthur F. **Tenants of The Almighty.** 1943.

Richmond, Mary E.
What is Social Case Work? An Introductory Description.
1922.

Riis, Jacob A. **The Children of the Poor.** 1892.

Rural Poor in the Great Depression: Three Studies. 1938.

Sedgwick, Theodore.
Public and Private Economy: Part I. 1836.

Smith, Reginald Heber. **Justice and the Poor.** 1919.

Sutherland, Edwin H. and Harvey J. Locke.
Twenty Thousand Homeless Men: A Study of Unemployed Men in the Chicago Shelters. 1936.

Tuckerman, Joseph.
On the Elevation of the Poor: A Selection From His Reports as Minister at Large in Boston. 1874.

Warner, Amos G. **American Charities.** 1894.

Watson, Frank Dekker.
The Charity Organization Movement in the United States: A Study in American Philanthropy. 1922.

Woods, Robert A., et al. **The Poor in Great Cities.** 1895.